To Janet,
enjoy!

Magic and Tragic Rosebud

Nancy Palker

M Palker

Lost Lake Folk Art
SHIPWRECKT BOOKS PUBLISHING COMPANY

IN®
DIE

Rushford, Minnesota

Front cover photos by Nancy Palker & Shipwreckt Books.
Cover, graphic & interior design by Shipwreckt Books.
Front cover includes a graphic layer depicting prayer
ribbons and tobacco tied to a memorial tree at Little
Bighorn Battlefield—from a photo by Judy McKeon.

For the Lakota People of Rosebud

Contents

Rosebud remembered

Even while still working at the Indian Health Service hospital on the Sioux reservation in Rosebud, South Dakota, the staff frequently talked about sharing the remarkable stories of our Rosebud experience in 1973-1974. For fresh college graduates embarking on nursing careers in the context of a different culture, it was a Big Adventure. The backdrop of the American civil rights movement added to the drama and richness of these times. But soon life got in the way, with busy careers and raising families. Our friendships have endured. It's pretty amazing that after all these years we still have such a bond. I think that speaks to the quality and intensity of the time we shared "in the trenches" of Rosebud.

Now, at last I have the time and presence of mind to put some of our stories on paper. I do not claim to be an expert in anything but my own memories, which at this point may be questionable at times. I appreciate the added input from those who shared these adventures, including Judy, Stephanie, Steve, Rose and Lorna who worked with me at Rosebud, and my friend Pam and brother Rick who dared to visit. I especially value the added information from Lorna and my newer Rosebud friends Maxine, Gina, Sandra, Cynthia and Jody.

So much history makes up the lifestyle, culture, and conditions in Rosebud that it is far beyond the scope of my memoir to include it all. Based on feedback from friends who read this work in progress, I have included some very basic information. The additional resource list offers an opportunity to expand one's understanding of the history and culture.

I consider it my privilege to share respectfully my perceptions of the Rosebud Brule Sioux/Lakota people, who have become very important to me. I freely admit that I was completely unaware and unprepared for the Rosebud experience. When I learned where we were going, I did do some reading. The orientation pamphlet sent to me by the Indian Health Service did not begin to tell the real story. I soon realized with surprise that the Lakota culture would be new and foreign to me. The Lakota Sioux actually had never even been on my radar in my previous Connecticut life, and so I hadn't really known what to expect. I had no point of reference.

I had no illusions of "saving the Indians." I'd always wanted to be a nurse so I could help others in general. I'd finished school and was there to cement my education with some practical experience. I thought I'd left the safe shores of home with a mind open to all possibilities. But as I dipped my toes into the wider world, I quickly found myself in over my head. The time at Rosebud has shaped my career, and over the years I have been carrying these people in my heart.

My original purpose in writing was to share these stories with family and friends, for both the entertainment value and to share a very pivotal time in my life. But a larger purpose emerged. The week that I began to write the first chapter of this book in 2014, I was in South Carolina for a family wedding when I met a man who had grown up in Rosebud. It was a fateful meeting, as it had taken me more than forty years to start writing the stories. We talked about Rosebud and my writing project, and he told me, "If enough people read it, maybe it could make a difference." My vision and focus widened.

While researching health statistics, I stumbled upon news of a current crisis at Rosebud hospital. Despite my concerted efforts, I had access to very limited information. It became clear that another visit to Rosebud was necessary. As I made travel plans, the largest peaceful gathering of Native people was building momentum in a months-long struggle to protect water and sacred land from the Dakota Access Oil Pipeline (DAPL). The book resonated more deeply with a momentum of its own.

The man I'd met in South Carolina, Ron Colombe, is also the one who described Rosebud fittingly as "magic and tragic." Perhaps Mr.

Colombe is right. If enough people learn about Rosebud, maybe some of the tragic things can finally change for the better. I hope the magic never gets lost.

Nancy Palker, RN, MSN—2018

1. U.S. Public Health Service Indian hospital in Rosebud, South Dakota, 1973.

Author's Note: This is a work of non-fiction. All of the events, encounters and conversations described are true to the best of the author's knowledge. In writing this book, I relied on my personal journal and researched facts, and I also consulted with several people mentioned in the book. Any errors are my own. I used real names whenever possible. Any profit the author makes from the book will be returned to the people of Rosebud.

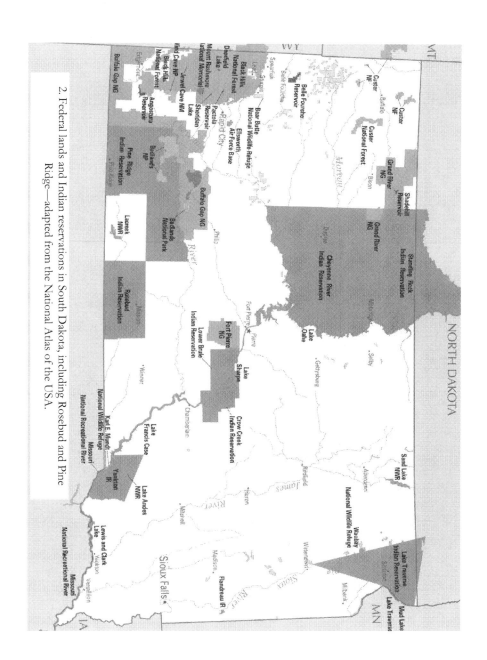

2. Federal lands and Indian reservations in South Dakota, including Rosebud and Pine Ridge—adapted from the National Atlas of the USA.

The Past – Adventure and Discovery

1. Welcome to Rosebud

RUTH. *WOWICAKE (WO-WEE-JAH-KEH)*. THAT WHICH IS REAL, THE WAY THE WORLD IS.

September 2016

Deep Breath.

The Lakota Studies sign at the entrance of *Sinte Gleska* University pointed toward two unmarked buildings.

We shrugged and chose the log cabin over its nondescript neighbor. I knocked, waited, and then opened the door to reveal a room with a few chairs, a folding table, a sink and countertop, but no people. I was feeling a bit anxious about our reception, based on our prior experiences in Rosebud.

"Hello," I called, reminding me of my first visit to the Rosebud Public Health Service Indian Hospital in 1973.

This time, a "Hello" was returned from a back room, followed by a pleasant dark-haired woman. "How can I help you?" she asked with a hint of a smile.

Another deep breath. The words came slowly as I carefully processed my thoughts to create a new path here.

"My name is Nancy Palker, and this is my friend Stephanie. We used to live in Rosebud. We worked as nurses at the hospital. It was back in the 1970s when all the American Indian Movement (AIM) activity and wild events were happening. I'm writing the stories of our experiences during that time. I'm looking for certain families to get their permission to use their names and photos in the book. I brought a list of the names I need so far. I thought I might hire a student to help me find and contact the families."

The woman introduced herself, Denise One Star, and immediately jotted contacts for several of the families. She came to Lame Deer's name on the list and directed us to talk to Maxine Bordeaux, who is this medicine man's daughter. She would have a lot of valuable information for us. Denise directed us to find Maxine's office on the other campus.

This visit was proving to be a contrast yet also an echo from our first time in Rosebud in August 1973 … We followed the trail of blood.

"Hello ... hello" we called, with no response. Our first glimpse of the Public Health Service Indian hospital in Rosebud, South Dakota already greatly differed from the busy hospitals back East. We had just been hired as newly graduated nurses, still waiting to hear whether we had passed our nursing board exams to become real RNs. Climbing up the small set of concrete steps to the old red brick building, through the peeling door frame of the quiet main entrance and down the drab narrow hallway, we had yet to see anyone. Then, following the sound of faint voices and blood splotches, we came upon the single large emergency room. Our first contact was Lucy Reifel, a local Sioux young woman still in medical school. We found her suturing a wounded man, the source of the bloody trail. She brusquely directed us upstairs to the medical-surgical unit to meet the nurses. We later learned that Lucy's uncle, Ben Reifel, was the first Lakota Indian Congressman, serving five terms from South Dakota.

My friend Judy Niederwerfer and I had just stopped by the reservation hospital unannounced, as we were not due to start work for another few weeks. We had graduated from the University of Connecticut School of Nursing in June, taken our nursing board exams in July, and quickly hit the road to see the USA. Neither of us had traveled much, and we both wanted to see what the world held for us outside of Connecticut. We had applied for several jobs west of the Mississippi, and the hospital in Rosebud (pop. 736) was the only one that would hire us together. We'd been unaware that the 54-bed rural hospital was supposed to have twenty-two RNs, but had only twelve, and six were brand new graduates with no experience just like us. Our new workplace was built of red brick in 1910, with a new wing in constructed in 1961.

Judy stood just a bit over my five feet four inches, with flashing brown eyes reflecting her endless energy and curiosity. Her interest in American Indians and the West was the driving force behind our fateful applications to the Indian Health Service. I'd gotten to know her late in our senior year of nursing school. Her enthusiasm was contagious, so I decided to follow her lead into the wild West. We had chosen careers in nursing to help people, but as white girls we had no illusions of "saving the Indians." Indeed, our careers were blank slates and we felt grateful for the opportunity to start our professions here in Rosebud.

Seeking adventure, we packed all our worldly possessions into Judy's brown Ford Maverick, called "Florence Nightingale," and left Connecticut to explore our country. We spent a month camping in a four by six-foot pup tent which, to our dismay, shrank in the rain. We had been planning to camp our way to the Pacific and then to end up in Rosebud for the first real job of our nursing careers. But after only a week into our month-long adventure, curiosity consumed us. We decided to stop by simply to check out the scene, as we'd had no real idea of what to expect.

A large dilapidated wooden "Welcome to Rosebud" sign had greeted us in the middle of the prairie. We'd seen no buildings or other signs, just tall sweet-smelling yellow grasses and big open sky. I guess this should have been our first clue as we viewed the vast, desolate Rosebud reservation.

The original Great Sioux Reservation of three million acres was created in 1868 by the Treaty of Fort Laramie. The Rosebud and Pine Ridge reservations in south central South Dakota were partitioned off in 1889 due to controversial treaty changes and claims, as gold was discovered in the Black Hills and homesteaders were pressing for additional grazing lands. Newer treaties nearly always reduced Indian land. Promises were repeatedly broken. Indians signed papers in languages they didn't understand. Not only did few speak English, but the legal terms were daunting. For comparison, the average American even now would have difficulty understanding the legalities of the Constitution or tax laws.

The Rosebud reservation in southern South Dakota now encompasses an area of 150 x 60 miles, or approximately one million acres of rolling grassland. The Lakota are one of the Original Seven Council Fires or bands, collectively known as the Sioux. The roughly 7500 people here in 1973 consist mostly of Brule or *Sicangu Oyate* and some *Oglala* people of the Lakota group. The Brule people got their name when, sadly, a group was burned after being caught in a grassland fire. They were known as the "Burnt Thigh" group, but the French traders called them Brule, meaning burned. *Sicangu Oyate* is the Lakota name.

These high plains all existed within the Lakota Sioux Nation, encompassing the land of Crazy Horse, Spotted Tail, and the Great Sioux Uprising. Over time, the indigenous people were persuaded to exchange land with the U.S. government in return for food, education, and health care in a series of controversial treaties. The Indians signed in good faith, although many did not understand the language or even the foreign concept of ownership. This complex and volatile aspect of American history holds far more information than can be covered here, but some will be visited later.

Meanwhile, the busy folks at the hospital welcomed Judy and me enthusiastically, if only briefly, in the bustle of the busy hospital unit. To our surprise and delight, they told us that our government housing was ready. The area offered no housing rentals for staff anywhere around here. Indeed, we would learn that the people of Rosebud themselves had few options, and many lived in overcrowded or unsafe conditions. So back we went to the Antelope Motel in the town of Mission, ten miles away. We checked back out, even though we had just checked in a couple of hours ago. The tired woman on duty looked devastated. The deserted parking lot told us that they didn't get much business there. The tiny dusty town consisted of Aboreszk's general store, the jail called "Heartbreak Hotel," the Starlite movie theatre, and the Western Bowl & Café. At the Farmer's Bank we met the teller, Alice Crabtree. She appeared to be in her forties, with short brown curly hair and glasses. Conversations with her were always long and personable whenever we went to deposit our paychecks. Direct deposit had yet to be invented, so we saw Alice every payday. We probably stood out from the average customer by depositing the entire check, with the benefit of free government housing and nothing much to spend money on at Rosebud. We had our electricity hooked up by joining the Cherry-Todd Co-op, and set up our phone account. Bison State Phone Company would benefit greatly from Judy's long nightly calls to her fiancé Russell, totaling $200 per month which was a small fortune in 1973. This covered only a land line, as other services such as cell, Wi-Fi, and cable did not yet exist. But the phone service would not start until we moved in, after we had completed our planned camping trip out West, in about three more weeks.

During our trip we phoned home every night or two, letting our parents know that we were ok and to share our latest discoveries. The only pay phone we found was on the sidewalk in the town of Mission. The receiver dangled forlornly in pieces, so our first task was to reassemble the phone. To our relief, when Judy put the receiver to her ear there was a dial tone. She fed in the quarters and called her parents. While Judy spoke with her dad, a rather unkempt man stumbled by, smelling strongly of alcohol.

He approached us saying, "Hey, are you girls?"

Though we were wearing shorts, I thought our gender was obvious. I replied, "Of course we're girls!"

Judy, listening to her dad and to me, quickly said, "No, we're not girls!"

I looked at her quizzically and said "Huh?"

Her dad was hearing both conversations and really wanted to know what was going on. Then it dawned on me. Ohhh, THAT kind of girls. "No, no, we're not." I'd immediately wanted to squeeze into the phone booth with Judy.

We found our housing, a new three-bedroom trailer in a small cluster across from the tribal buffalo herd. We met our pretty dark-haired neighbor Susan Beeson, from the trailer next door. She had worked previously in Chicago but had been in Rosebud for a while. Wow. An experienced nurse. Her adorable two-year-old foster son, Freddie Thundershield accompanied her, in constant motion. After spending time in our shrinking pup tent, the trailer seemed like a palace. However, we soon learned that after sitting out in the Dakota summer sun all day, the metal trailer could easily reach a temperature above 120 degrees. Opening the door, the heat blasted out to greet us, and it would take a half hour to air it out before we could tolerate going inside. Everything was spiffy new, but the trailer vibrated when we walked through, feeling less than solid. Our dented and sooty camping mess kits and cooking pot contrasted with the gleaming new stove and bright yellow kitchen, but they did the job until we could go shopping.

Once most of our extra stuff was secured in our trailer, we set out again from Rosebud for the second part of our camping adventure, to the Pacific coast. Following our 1973 McDonald's map of the U.S. which marked all the McDonalds, we stopped for Big Macs and fries whenever possible. We must have known they would be in short supply once we settled into extremely rural Rosebud. Fast food was still a relative novelty in 1973.

On we trekked into more new territory. We survived "the plague of the day," including black flies, mosquitoes, a tornado, a dust storm, sandstorm, and a blowout tire at 70 mph on the Utah Salt Flats. We visited Yellowstone Park, the Tetons, Little Big Horn, Glacier Park, the Grand Canyon, Bryce Park, Zion Park, and the Painted Desert. We went whitewater rafting, hiked up waterfalls, were chased by bears, dipped our toes in the foggy Pacific, and stood barefoot in the summer snows of the Rockies. Truly we did see firsthand what lay beyond our tiny home state, and we fell in love with our great land and its people. Four weeks after leaving our homes in Connecticut, and three weeks after our pop-in to see the hospital, we returned to Rosebud, starting our illustrious careers in the decrepit and horribly understaffed Public Health Service Indian hospital.

Although part of the red brick building was actually condemned, it remained in use, without any alternative Indian hospital for more than a hundred miles. The U.S. Government is mandated by treaty to provide healthcare for those with a certain fraction of Indian blood. Each tribe determines the required percentage, according to David Treuer in his book *Rez Life*. At that time, the Indians were only eligible for free health care at Indian hospitals, and no other ethnic group could be treated there. Rosebud Hospital was often so overcrowded that there were patients lying on stretchers lining the band-aid brown hallways.

By 1973 the civil rights movement of the sixties had reached this remote area. Like the urban Black Panthers, the militant American Indian Movement (AIM) actively and adamantly sought dignity, equality, and justice. That Spring, the neighboring Pine Ridge Reservation had experienced a violent siege of 71 days at Wounded Knee. We hadn't heard much about it back in Connecticut before we had naively left home, as we'd been studying for exams, planning our trip, and then traveling. So, we were surprised to find such great unrest and racial tension here. It was definitely the Wild West, with shootouts, outlaws, and an FBI blockade, on a background of crushing poverty and rich cultural traditions. Pow wows with richly adorned costumes and fragrant buffalo stew, sweat lodges, and medicine men were part of everyday life. I'd had no idea what I was getting into.

With great excitement on our first day of work in August of 1973, Judy and I drove the 10 miles from our government trailer in the town of Mission, cruising into the sunrise across rolling grassland, singing "O What a Beautiful Morning" and "When It's Roundup Time in Rosebud," a cowboy tune Judy had tweaked a little that seemed perfect for the occasion. Arriving at Rosebud hospital we met the acting Director of Nursing (DON) Sister Carmela, who was orienting the new DON, Montilou along with Judy and me. Montilou was from

Texas, and true to the big Texas stereotype, she sported a generous frame with large features and poufy brown hair. She drove a huge brown Ford Brougham, and it really did have longhorns on the grille, a true symbol of a Texan in those days. She had been an army nurse and appeared to be in her fifties.

We spent our first formative hour learning the Public Health Service chain of command. Welcome to the government indeed. Then the DONs had to go to another meeting, so they told us to look around the medical-surgical unit. The busy head nurse, petite white-haired Mrs. Heth said, "The best way to learn is by doing," and promptly assigned us a few patients each.

My first patient said she needed a bedpan, so I went down the hall looking for one. I ran into Dr. Lenz, who said he needed help with an exam. I tried to explain that I was looking for a bedpan, but he overrode that task and urgently recruited me for his patient's exam. As I was exiting the exam room later to resume the bedpan search, I heard the DONs returning down the hall saying, "...maybe one of those two new nurses..." Naively, I walked into the hall anyway.

They said to me, "Nancy, how would you like to go on an ambulance ride?" As I hesitated and started to explain about the bedpan search, they interrupted, saying "It's part of your orientation."

"Well, if it's part of my orientation, sure..." Hah! So much for the poor woman waiting for the bedpan ... we scrambled to take Quannah Crow Dog, a seven- month-old baby in respiratory distress, on a 350-mile trip to a medical center in Rapid City, SD. My nursing education had not included ambulance rides. I was alone with the driver, so my "orientation" was apparently to wing it, an exercise I discovered would be often repeated at Rosebud. The ambulance supplied oxygen and suction, and when I asked the driver how to use it, he said he was just a driver and didn't know about equipment or protocols. I figured out the equipment, monitored and fed the baby, sang, prayed, and rocked him in my arms. He slept, as we hurried over sometimes rugged dirt lanes, stopping for occasional cows in the road on our eight-hour journey through the endless rolling hills of the prairie. Thankfully, Quannah kept breathing as we made our way and I safely put the baby into the hands of the medical staff.

Upon my return to Rosebud, earning two hours of overtime, I was told that the baby was the son of Leonard Crow Dog, a fierce leader in the militant American Indian Movement, and a medicine man himself. When I met him later I was impressed by his strong and imposing presence. He had told hospital staff that if anything happened to his baby, he would kill the one responsible. We later learned that the baby had tuberculosis, as did so many of our patients. Quannah returned a couple of months later in improved health, and so thankfully his father allowed me to keep my health too.

We met medicine men with whom we occasionally collaborated. Many patients would come in with their medicine bags, little rawhide pouches of amulets for healing. Sadly, despite all of our best efforts, many of the tiny bags were easily lost when patients were bathed, and gowns and linens were changed. We often heard of sweat lodges and other traditional healing ceremonies in the community. It was an honor for me to take care of John Strike, a local medicine man, shortly before he died. Even though his strength was waning, his spirit was so powerful that it was a comfort for me just being in the same room with him.

Later that fall, baby Quannah Crow Dog was back in the hospital. While we took care of him with antibiotics and IVs, his father chanted and covered the crib with feathers, rocks, and beads. Quannah again recovered, and we as young RNs learned a valuable lesson as we expanded our definition of medicine.

It was such an intense time in a desolate area, within a fascinating culture of strong and colorful traditions. Like dry sponges from Connecticut suburbia, we readily soaked up experiences and knowledge. But so much more would come, both magic and tragic.

Wowicake.

3. Judy greeting the first Rosebud sign, 1973

4. Main road through Rosebud, 1973

2. Pow wow

PERSEVERANCE. *WOWACINTANKA (WO-WAH-CHIN-TAN-GAH).*
TO PERSIST, TO STRIVE IN SPITE OF DIFFICULTIES.

The rhythmic drum beat drew me in like a communal heartbeat, so loud that I could feel it in the center of my chest. Several men from the Parmalee Singers gathered around the enormous skin drum, beating in unison. Then they began singing, chanting, and wailing together in the Lakota language, as well as in syllables that evoked a sense of timeless tradition and power (*Hey ya hey ya ho* …). In bright colorful feathers the fancy dancers began to move, jingling armlets and anklets accenting the drumbeat as they danced. Feathers perched on their heads and backs, and sometimes dancers displayed arm and leg plumage too. Many groups wore distinctive outfits to identify their tribe or nation. Spectators and dancers awaiting their turns stood or sat beneath the log and branch bower encircling the dance field. This bower provided welcome shade in the dry heat, often over 100 degrees, baking the fragrant prairie grass in the summer sun. Some women wore dark blue dresses trimmed in clattering cowrie shells. Many dancers wore extensively beaded buckskin outfits, some decorated with colorful woven porcupine quills or fur. Some even donned bright war paint and carried tomahawks. Most women dancers wrapped themselves in embroidered and fringed dancing shawls. I saw dancers of all ages, from kids who had just learned to walk to older folks who'd been dancing all their lives. Spectators usually wore jeans and casual shirts with cowboy boots, and a few wore moccasins.

The songs and dances celebrated a wide range of topics: a traditional rain dance to pray for rain, prayers to honor *Wakan Tanka*— the Great Spirit, rabbit and bear dances for a good hunt. Pow wows, or *wacipi*, could mark a variety of occasions, such as a birth, a naming, a marriage, becoming a man or a woman, adoption or *hunka* ceremonies, celebrations to welcome someone home from a long absence, school graduations, or contests for prizes.

The tempting aromas of buffalo stew and fry bread with berry sauce wafted by. I'm sure the musicians and dancers worked up hearty appetites, as did those of us watching the highly skilled performers. The extraordinarily high energy fancy dancers jumped and whirled into a frenzy and blur of color. Other dances were more sedate; the rabbit dancers bobbed and walked in rhythm and a simple pattern. I know this first-hand, as I was the only blonde dancing in several pow wows, but more on this later.

This pow wow was the big annual Rosebud Fair, with performers from as far away as Oklahoma and Arizona. Many camped in RVs, tents, and tipis beside the dance area for the multi-day affair. The competition for prize money was fierce, especially on an impoverished reservation with 70 percent unemployment.

Many beautiful handicrafts and dance outfits were on parade. The local artisans brought their signature fine beadwork, quillwork, Morningstar quilts, and local pottery. The Navajo people proudly displayed their silver and turquoise jewelry and woven hand- dyed blankets. I heard an assortment of hand-carved flutes and pipes. Looking back, it would have been the perfect time to sell all these things, but I can't recall seeing organized vendor booths. Capitalism had not really arrived at Rosebud in 1973. There was a new craft co-op tucked away in the tiny center of Rosebud with beadwork supplies and local pottery, but it was not clearly marked, and not advertised. People did work diligently all year to make beautiful dance outfits. They had guilds for special skills; men made feather bustles while women sewed and beaded the buckskin outfits and accessories. The Lakota tradition and their world view promotes giving and trading over selling and sharing over ownership. Maybe the generations of oppression had squashed the energy, ambition, and hope needed to make a profit. But, at least back then it was not about making money. It was about expressing and celebrating a once endangered identity. Perhaps it was a combination of factors. But I'm pretty sure that if all these treasures had been openly available for sale, I'd have spent some of my first real pay checks to buy gifts for family, friends, and myself.

As we delved deeper into the culture, meeting more and more people, their names truly fascinated me. For many years it was illegal for these Lakota to use their own names, or any traditional practices, in an attempt by our government to promote assimilation and eliminate the culture entirely. Not so long ago people risked their lives for these names. Sometimes names were given in secret traditional ceremonies, which were often followed by a pow wow and "giveaway," where the family gave generous gifts to all the guests to thank them for their attention, support, participation and good wishes. Giveaways, like pow wows, are associated with all kinds of special events, as a way of sharing the joy, honor, or sorrow of the occasion. Traditional names may be given by healers and can carry a spiritual meaning, "almost like a godparent, giving advice and help. Names can be given at times of significance and not only at birth. When you take part in a naming you are giving a part of your soul to this person being named" according to David Treuer in his book *Rez Life*.

Ollie Pretty Bird was a nursing aide who taught me how to do beadwork in exchange for knitting & crochet lessons. My lessons included making belts, bracelets, hatbands and barrettes on a beading loom, as well as daisy chain necklaces and spiral earrings, using the tiniest fine local beads and needles. Ollie's beading skills far exceeded my beginner knitting and crochet level, so I always felt badly that I got the better end of that exchange. Reserved and well respected in the community, she would later work as a cultural consultant for the 1990s Oscar-winning movie *Dances with Wolves*. I was honored that Ollie allowed me to enter her private and guarded world, and I enjoyed her company immensely.

Richard Fool Bull, a soft-spoken dignified man in his nineties, came to the hospital one day selling some beautiful cedar courting flutes that he had made. With brightly painted duck heads trimmed in rawhide and feathers, the flutes' haunting sounds as he played were as beautiful as their appearance. I couldn't resist buying one. He said that he was the last one to make these distinctive kinds of flutes, and he was worried the tradition would die. They had been used when families shared tipis, without privacy. The average Lakota tipi (which means "they live there") was made of sixteen to twenty long poles in a conical framework, covered with twenty or so tanned hides. This formed one oval-shaped room for an average of seven people. If a young man liked a young woman, he would stand outside the tipi and play the flute. If the woman appreciated the serenade, she would come outside wrapped in her blanket to listen. If she fancied the man, she would invite him into her blanket. I asked Mr. Fool Bull to teach me to play, as the flutes' voices were so lovely, each one unique. The flute was more than a piece of visual art, it was a fine instrument that deserved to be heard. He wouldn't take money, so I paid him with squash from my garden. I tried to understand his melodies, but he never played them the same way twice. It was only years later that I came to understand how he played from his inner spirit. My personal life has been too busy so far to find the inner peace to play his or my own spirit songs. But I recently found a local group who play Native flutes who might teach me, though I did not see any flutes constructed or decorated quite like mine. I also learned much later that Fool Bull was one of the few survivors of the original Wounded Knee massacre in 1890.

George Whirlwind Soldier was a physician's assistant student, training with one of the Rosebud doctors. George was named after his grandfather, who had killed an army officer in one of the battles in the 1890s. He had taken the dead officer's uniform and would put it on, whistling and beckoning to foot soldiers, leading them into an Indian ambush. Then he would ride off and remove the uniform and disappear, earning his name, Whirlwind Soldier. The younger George later became one of the most beloved long-term staff members at the hospital, noted for his very thoughtful and caring nature.

Thomas Wolf Guts had been my patient briefly, and I later learned that he'd been a code talker in WWII.

Leonard Crow Dog describes in his book *Crow Dog* how his ancestor got his name. His great-grandfather nearly died in the desert and was saved by a crow and a coyote. He took the name of Crow Coyote. But his name was misunderstood by census takers and became Crow Dog.

According to Sprague in his book *Rosebud Sioux*, John Fire (also called Lame Deer) had an unusual name origin. His father was called Let Them Have Enough when they moved to Rosebud. During the name registration he was told that his name was too long. That same day a fire suddenly broke out at the registration site and so they named him John Fire. His daughter Maxine told me that when people came to him for his traditional healing skills, he was one of the first medicine men to encourage them also to use the white medicine at Rosebud hospital as well. Maxine would pick medicinal plants for Lame Deer to use in his healing ceremonies.

Some more of the colorful names of people we met include Doreen Singing Goose, Amelia He Dog, Wanda Big Crow, Alice Four Horns, Mr. Shot with Two Arrows, Pauline Never Misses a Shot, the Hollow Horn Bear family, Joe Eagle Elk, and Norman Short Bull.

In a naïve attempt to get into the spirit of things, Judy and I invented local-sounding names as we worked: Nancy Rock-a-Baby in the nursery and Judy Shot-in-the-Ass when giving medications on the medical-surgical unit. However, one of the local LPNs, Claudia, called us "Honkers" (Honkeys) because we were white. The Lakota word for whites is *wasichu*, which we heard often. We had been told that *wasichu* means "thing that never goes away," but recently it was explained to me that it translates to "fat takers."

We had yet to understand and appreciate the struggle, sacrifice and triumph within the proud Lakota names. We would not have presumed to invent names for ourselves had we understood the profound cultural value.

A few weeks after the big summer pow wow, lots of interest buzzed when the movie *Billy Jack* came to the Starlight theatre in Mission, months after it had opened elsewhere. Judy and I knew it was about an Indian, and so we went to see it as one of our few recreational diversions. We were impressed by the theatre itself with glow in the dark stars on the ceiling. A small twelve-inch TV screen on the stage showed cartoons instead of previews on the big screen behind it. As we settled in to watch the movie, a handful of folks seated behind us began calling us "Honkeys" and threatened to beat us up in the parking lot after the movie. The film's plot featured an Indian Green Beret vet who had become a pacifist, but he was forced to fight to defend his tribe. As the movie progressed and the plot intensified, the threats from behind us escalated. We decided to leave before the end to avoid the threatened beating. We had seen enough brutal beatings at the hospital to have faith in their ability to carry out the threat. As someone who had been so naïve to have never even considered Native Americans as a race so different from my own, it was a revelation to me to be hated and threatened for my looks alone. These people sitting behind me didn't even know me as a person, or that I had come to give care at the hospital. It opened my eyes to the ugly world of blind bigotry. I gained some empathy, and a glimmer of insight into a lifelong experience for far too many people then and now.

I had learned some of the local history, though, and much justification lurked behind this hostility. First came the explorers bringing new diseases to ravage the Native populations. Then, in the 1800s the U.S. policy of extermination encouraged killing all indigenous people to make way for white settlers. If the people couldn't be killed, soldiers and settlers killed the buffalo to remove the Indian food supply, and source of their clothing, shelter and spiritual strength. The army actually gave Indian survivors some blankets infected with smallpox, as they knew the Indians had no resistance to this disease. When Columbus landed, there were about twelve million Native Americans. In 1970 only about 800,000 remained, according to Wikipedia's Historical Racial and Ethnic Demographics of the U.S. Populations were wiped out by massacre, disease, and malnutrition. Treaties were revised whenever minerals or other value were found on the Indian land, with those prime areas given to the white settlers. Since the Indian culture had previously included no concept of owning land, they were often confused by all these treaties in a foreign language with foreign ideas, but they soon understood the threats to their existence. General Custer more than met his match with chiefs Crazy Horse, Spotted Tail and Sitting Bull and their warriors. According to the 1972 Public Health Service orientation booklet, these Sioux are "recognized as the greatest light cavalry ever organized and the only nation ever to put the U.S. Army into full retreat."

However, the press of white settlers persisted. The survivors were confined to ever-shrinking reservations as treaties were revised and broken. Once the reservations were established, a great effort followed to "convert" and "assimilate" the Indian survivors into the dominant culture by forcibly removing the children to harsh boarding schools, forbidding them to speak their language or practice their traditions. These schools were a wedge that split many families apart. The children were stripped of any remnant of their tribal dress or language. Even handmade dolls were taken from little children and siblings were separated. Their long hair, which is a source of spiritual strength, was cut. Military-style uniforms replaced their soft handmade buckskin clothes. Family visits were banned for long stretches of time, sometimes years. The children were punished severely or horribly abused for any infraction, or sometimes for no reason at all. When the children returned home, they often suffered the dilemma of being caught between two cultures. They were not welcome in the white settlements, nor did they really fit back with their people, where many traditions were still kept. As Joseph Marshall recounts in his book *The Lakota Way*, when resistance ceased to be an option, there was no other choice but to reach deep inside and fight with the only remaining weapon: spiritual strength. Native beliefs were ridiculed and reviled. The assimilation program sought to dissolve Native identities in the boarding schools, outlawing the language and traditions in an intensive effort to tear away their culture.

When children were forbidden to speak their language at these schools, wise grandmothers told them to "whisper" to keep it alive. When the church and police came to their tipis to convert them to Christianity, some medicine men would hide some of their sacred pipes and medicine bundles, quietly guarding the old ways.

U.S. policies further diluted the power of families, ancestors, and ties to the land and nature by resettling in cities with promises of jobs. But cities also gave access to new information and resources, resulting in the formation of some intertribal and political alliances as these people intermingled with others in the growing civil rights movement.

The 1960s finally saw an end to the boarding schools and a growing interest in reclaiming the old traditions. 1978 brought the American Indian Religious Freedom Act. Today, the people of Rosebud continue to practice many of the traditions and beliefs of their ancestors. Like many who have adapted to survive, Rosebud's people have become reserved and self-contained. Unfortunately, there also is much evidence of damage from generations of oppression, struggle and hardship.

The pow wow experience could offer many faces. Rose is a nurse who came to the reservation hospital in December of 1973. She relates this story of the following year's big summer Rosebud Fair:

"It was Pow wow time, a convenient time for mothers to bring their children to the hospital near the fairgrounds for such things as high fevers and bad coughs. The emergency clinic stood at the end of a long first floor hallway. On one side, four exam rooms with connecting doors opened to the main hallway. Across the hall was a large emergency room, lined with supply shelves. In the center stood an exam table but the room was large enough to accommodate a second and third stretcher, if necessary.

"The first-floor entrances to the hospital were locked after regular day hours. The nurse from the second-floor medical unit was expected to answer the doorbell when anyone came to the emergency door. On this particular night, I was the nurse on the second floor. I had completed my rounds and was preparing to do chores when the emergency doorbell rang, just after midnight. I went down and answered the door to find four mothers with their assorted children.

"I placed each family in an exam room, assessed the children, and, according to standing orders, determined what medications they all needed. I left the area to gather medications at the pharmacy. Upon returning to the first exam room, I found it empty. I proceeded through the connecting doors to the second and third rooms, which were also empty; so on through the connecting door to the fourth room. There I found all four mothers and their children, huddled together. All had looks of terror in their eyes. I asked what was wrong but no one answered. I asked again and one brave mother raised a wavering finger pointing across toward the emergency room. I crossed the hallway and passed through the ER doors. What impressed me first was the blood everywhere—on the floor, on some of the shelves and equipment that had been pulled down and opened, and especially on two men. One was stretched out on the exam table and the other slumped in a wheelchair. A third man, also somewhat bloodied, was pacing the room. Two women also seemed to have some blood spattered on them but were otherwise unharmed. Most, if not all of them had been drinking based on the alcohol aroma that permeated the air. I recognized the men as members of the militant American Indian Movement activist group, AIM.

"The man who was pacing saw me and walked toward me with a six-inch hunting knife in hand. He placed the tip of the blade under my chin and said," If he dies, you die."

"Shaking in my figurative boots, I said with as much calm as I could muster, 'Well, let me examine them first.' I wasn't sure which 'he' I was to keep alive, but I went straight-away to the man on the exam table. His face was a bloody puffy mess and his eyes were swollen shut. As I was taking vital signs and doing some neuro checks, I asked one of the nearby ladies what had happened.

"She replied in a surly fashion, 'What does it look like happened?'

"Wanting to sound like my question was perfectly reasonable, I replied, 'It looks like he got the hell beat out of him, but with what? A lead pipe, a baseball bat, a fist?'

"She said it was a fist fight. I determined that the first patient looked worse than he actually was—thank goodness—and went to examine the patient in the wheelchair. He seemed to be fairly stable also. The man pacing the room declined an exam. I explained that I was going to go to the next room and call the doctor, which I did. I also called Mr. Arnold, the Assistant Director of Nursing and a nurse himself, and begged him to please come in. I thought the doctor might appreciate a second man as back-up. I knew I wanted one. Mr. Arnold readily agreed to come.

"I went back to the ER and began cleaning blood from the two patients. Soon, the doctor and Mr. Arnold arrived and took over. I returned to the waiting mothers and their children, quickly dispensed medications with directions, and walked them out of the hospital. They were so relieved to get safely away!

"Then it was back to the emergency room. The doctor and Mr. Arnold seemed to have everything pretty much in hand. I started the paperwork and assisted as needed. With all the attention they had been getting, the two patients started to rally. After the suturing and bandaging was completed, they refused admission. All five left, stumbling out into the quiet of the night.

"The doctor looked at Mr. Arnold and me and said, 'Well, thanks for your help.' And he left us. Mr. Arnold, bless his heart, stayed to help me clean the area and make everything ready for the next emergency, whenever it might happen. Then he, too, left for the night.

"I returned to the relative safety of the second- floor medical unit to find that everything had remained calm, thanks to the experienced care of the two nursing assistants. I was so glad when the morning sun broke over the hill and the day staff started to arrive. I went home to bed and rest, so I could be prepared for whatever the following night might bring."

Rose's story presents another person's view of the pow wow experience.

Meanwhile, I had been thinking about the captivating pow wow music that had moved and stirred my spirit recently, and I realized how much I missed having music in my life. I had grown up in a musical family and had been singing from an early age. I missed being part of a musical community, so I enrolled in a Lakota music class at the brand new *Sinte Gleska* Community College in Rosebud. The school had been started so that students could learn near home, as a reaction and antidote to those boarding schools. It offered classes in Lakota traditions and history, as well as nursing, business, and other disciplines. It was named after Chief Spotted Tail, as his name in Lakota is *Sinte Gleska*. I was excited to try the class. Though I was the only non-native in the class of less than ten, I loved to sing and my voice carried the Lakota words and melodies loud and clear. Our teacher Ben Black Bear also taught us a few simple dance steps for the more sedate songs. His daughter Sandra recently told me that Ben and his wife were so passionate about passing on Lakota traditions that they would teach classes in beading, crafts, and music wherever they could find a space.

After a couple of weeks, another local woman began coming to the class, but not to participate. For several weeks in a row during the entire class she just sat and glared at me as I sang. I recognized her from working in the hospital as the one who usually brought the breakfast trays. She had wanted me to help her pass out the trays, but I was unable to help her since I was the only nurse to pour and pass morning meds to my 25 patients at that time. I had explained this to her several times, but still she seemed to resent the fact that I couldn't help her and the other aides. Now it appeared she had come specifically to harass me silently in class. After several weeks of practice, our teacher Ben Black Bear decided our class was ready and assigned us to attend a small local pow wow.

Actually, we were expected not just to attend but to perform. We'd been learning to sing the Lakota National Anthem along with other songs and the steps to a rabbit dance. My friend and coworker, Lorna Her Many Horses told me I needed a dancing shawl, as the women dancers all wore them for this type of event. Lorna was from Rosebud, and her husband Leo also worked at the hospital. They had six boys, and then a daughter named simply Baby Girl. Their son Chico was a fancy dancer and had won many competitions. She generously offered to lend me one of her beautifully embroidered and fringed dancing shawls. So off I went to the pow wow, a bit nervous as the only blonde performer in this time of extreme racial tensions. I didn't make many mistakes nor any obvious goofs.

Several days after that pow wow, one morning at work I saw the dietary aide passing breakfast trays. Miraculously, this time she smiled and asked, "Are you goin' to the pow wow at He Dog next Saturday?" Wow! I was floored by such a turnaround in attitude. I wasn't consciously trying to be an ambassador. I really only had planned to learn and enjoy some music. But at some other times too, with patients in the emergency room and when out at Chases Women Lake, some of the initial mistrust and hostility dropped away when folks recognized me as the blonde in the pow wow. I credit the transformative power of music and an open spirit.

Wowacintanka.

5. Rosebud Fair Pow Wow, 1973

6. Rosebud Fair Pow Wow boys, 1973

7. Rosebud Fair Pow Wow dancers, 1973

3. The Shooting

ACRIFICE. *ICICUPI (EE-CHEE-CHU-PEE)*. TO GIVE OF
ONESELF, AN OFFERING.

"Clyde Bellecourt's been shot!" yelled Catherine
Vallandra, our nursing assistant.

"Who's Clyde Bellecourt?" I asked.

"One of the big AIM guys, and there's a whole bunch of 'em heading this way!"

That early fall morning our routines quickly fell into chaos on the busy medical-surgical unit as an all-star AIM mob crowded our hallway. Dennis Banks, Russell Means, Leonard Crow Dog, and about twenty-five warriors blocked our path and took food from trays as we tried to distribute lunch to our patients. I was appalled by this behavior, plus feeling outnumbered and intimidated in the crush of men in the hallway. But mostly I felt frustrated that our patients were not getting all the care they needed. However, the hospital had no visitor's cafeteria, nor do I remember a waiting room. There was no cafe in town; the nearest one was ten miles away in Mission. I guess that under the circumstances the rowdy group of warriors might not have had too many options while they waited for news of their friend Clyde Bellecourt's condition.

Someone said that Carter Camp, an AIM security guard, was the one who had shot Bellecourt in the abdomen. I later learned that the shooting was a result of a long-simmering feud, compounded by the effects of alcohol, according to Russell Means in his autobiography, *Where White Men Fear to Tread*. The FBI set up a blockade around Rosebud for several days to try to catch Mr. Camp. With few roads, and only 70 miles of them paved in 9,000 square miles of reservation, it seemed to me that a road block was of limited value with so much open land for escape. We saw the FBI guys all over the place as we went to and from work.

The shooting was linked to the 71-day Wounded Knee siege that had taken place the past spring, where several people had died in the chaos of what had begun as a seemingly noble cause.

Clyde Bellecourt had co-founded the American Indian Movement with Dennis Banks and others in 1968, seeking dignity and respect for Native Americans. According to Russell Means, AIM's objectives were to protest the U.S. government's treatment of Native Americans and to demand that the government honor its treaties with Indian tribes. Bellecourt had been the group's first leader. Remarkably, the group had been conceived in a Minnesota prison, where Natives were routinely subject to extensive police brutality (Indians.org). A top priority was to end the brutality. Many of the Indian men had been nearly destroyed by the hatred and racism they had faced, according to Alysa Landry. She sheds additional light on this history in her excellent article in the online journal *Indian Country Today*, May 8, 2017 on the forty-fourth anniversary of the end of the Wounded Knee occupation. She reports that at that time Natives across the country battled abuse in boarding schools or left reservations to chase government promises of education and jobs in urban areas. As Natives arrived in cities, they faced widespread racism, especially among the white police forces. "People were beaten down and afraid to speak out. We had to create an organization to represent the people," says Bellecourt in his 2013 book, *We Are Still Here: A Photographic History of the American Indian Movement.*

Like the militant Black Panthers of the late 1960s, AIM in the 1970s often took extreme measures in their own civil rights struggles. Alysa Landry reports that AIM was labeled as one of the fifty worst terrorist groups in the U.S. They had occupied fifty-four federal facilities, including Mt. Rushmore, Alcatraz, the Bureau of Indian Affairs in Washington, D.C., and a replica of the Mayflower in Plymouth, Massachusetts. Banks proclaimed, "AIM is the new warrior class of this century, bound by the bond of the drum, who vote with their bodies instead of their mouths; their business is hope."

Leonard Crow Dog notes in his autobiography, *Crow Dog*, that "There was a whispering in the air, a faint drumbeat, a hoof beat. It became a roar carried by the four winds: 'A nation is coming; the eagle brought the message.' What was coming called itself AIM, the American Indian Movement." In October of 1972 AIM had organized the Trail of Broken Treaties. This was a caravan starting on the west coast, stopping to pray at Indian massacre sites. They headed for Washington D.C. to meet with President Nixon's representatives to discuss ending the corruption and mismanagement in the Bureau of Indian Affairs, part of the Department of the Interior. Some felt that the BIA represented all that was wrong with the government's Indian policy. AIM had twenty key points of contention related to treaty violations, Indian rights and self-government. After traveling for a month, the peaceful caravan of about 1500 people from 200 tribes stretched several miles long by the time it reached Washington, DC the week before the Presidential election. The original intention was peaceful and friendly, to meet with senators and congressmen from their states. They planned to offer frybread to the representatives and fancy dancing for the public. Organizers had promised the group food and shelter. But the visitors were herded into the unheated basement of a church that was abandoned, except for rats, according to Crow Dog's account. Communications broke down, which delayed the meeting with government reps. On November 2, 1972, the frustrated AIM leaders presented themselves, and then refused to leave the comfort of the heated BIA offices. This frustration and anger quickly escalated into a seven-day armed takeover and occupation of the BIA. Crow Dog captures some of the essential sentiment of AIM:

"We are not the BIA's wards anymore. Enough. Enough. Enough … Hey white America, listen to me. Before you came here we had no lawyers, no penitentiaries, no foster homes, no old age homes, no mental institutions, no psychiatric clinics, no taxes, no TV, no telephones. We had no crime or madness or drugs. Look at these wonderful things you brought us. You call it 'civilization' because a stupid and greedy man called Columbus thought he was in India when he landed here. He did not discover America. We had been here for tens of thousands of years. We are the landlords and one day we'll come to collect the rent."

Although the takeover was resolved with the U.S. government agreeing to review and address the twenty key points of contention, to this day none of the twenty points have yet been resolved.

In early 1973, AIM was invited by a local civil rights group to the Pine Ridge Reservation, which neighbors Rosebud. Specifically, this time they were protesting racial discrimination in border towns and by law enforcement, as well as the poor living conditions, local tribal corruption, and federal government policies. Major U.S. policies have included the mass killings of Native people and then the slaughter of their sacred buffalo in the name of *Manifest Destiny,* to clear the way for white settlers to claim their lands. One example is the 1830 Indian Removal Act, which was designed to relocate and confine Natives onto reservations. On the Trail of Tears alone, four thousand Cherokee people died of cold, hunger, and disease. The June 29, 2008

Washington *Post* summarized later policies: "...for much of the preceding century the nation's indigenous people had been forcibly assimilated. They'd been legally denied the right to practice their religious rituals and were herded into government boarding schools where white administrators cut the students' long hair and forbade them to speak their native languages."

The Pine Ridge reservation's unrest brought to a head more than a hundred years of racial tension and government corruption. Crow Dog reports that Pine Ridge's tribal chairman Dick Wilson was elected by fraudulent votes and "ran the tribe like a dictator, using tribal funds to hire a private army of killers to intimidate his opposition." Impeachment was not an option. Russell Means states that in 1973-75 under Wilson, Pine Ridge became the world's homicide capital and was known locally as the Reign of Terror.

AIM led an occupation on February 27, 1973, and seized the trading post in the same impoverished village that was the site of the massacre of 1890, in Wounded Knee on the Pine Ridge reservation. They cut the phone lines and ran the BIA police out of town. FBI agents and U.S. Marshalls surrounded the town with the National Guard. Several people were killed and injured in a number of gun battles. This occupation of two hundred Sioux attracted supporters from dozens of other tribes and civil rights groups, and some global attention to generations of mistreatment by federal and local agencies.

Kevin McKiernan was the only journalist imbedded with AIM, as he had walked from neighboring Rosebud and sneaked past the federal blockade in the last weeks of the occupation. He says in Landry's article, "Wounded Knee was a line in the sand. Death was a price they were willing to pay."

Many, especially tribal elders, thought that the occupation was disrespectful. They preferred to work with tribal and federal governments to solve longstanding problems. By the end of the occupation, Landry states, most people realized that they had accomplished little working through the system. "This became a beacon for change. Wounded Knee gave people pride, hope, and a different view of themselves."

McKiernan reports that food and medical supplies were banned. Supplies dwindled as the occupation stretched on. Clyde Bellecourt, Russell Means, and Carter Camp held a meeting with a representative of the U.S. President to negotiate an end to the 71 day siege on May

8th. The government delegation agreed to examine the problems at issue. AIM agreed to surrender, as the Sioux national anthem played. However, the AIM leaders were ultimately notified that only Congress can change the laws, and no further action was taken on the problems. About twelve hundred people were arrested, but many were acquitted because of evidence that the FBI had manipulated key witnesses.

Wounded Knee today still represents a troubled history and people who would do anything to incite change. McKiernan states, "The purpose of the 1890 massacre was … an object lesson delivered on a large scale. Then there were dead years when Indian people won the race to the bottom in every possible sociological statistic. That changed with the occupation of Wounded Knee."

With this backdrop of recent activity, Judy and I arrived in neighboring Rosebud a few months later, in August. We had heard very little about the situation as we had been wrapped in our own world, studying for our exams and preparing for our travels, and then camping in remote areas. We walked into this place and time, far beyond unprepared, and we found all of Rosebud to be a steep learning curve.

AIM was indeed a breath of fresh air to many Indians, bringing some hope and attention to problems in the community, as well as empowering some positive changes. However, not everyone was inspired. Many Indians and whites saw AIM as a group of bullies and thugs.

Steve Tosi, a young doctor with caring green eyes and an easy smile had come to work in Rosebud as an alternative to the draft during the Vietnam war. He was training two local physician assistants, Charlie White and George Whirlwind Soldier, who were attending the University of North Dakota at that time. As part of his mentoring, he had to attend an occasional meeting at the university, and due to the great distance, the university would send a plane for him. During this tense time, someone shot at the plane, and although nobody was injured, it never landed or returned.

Dr. Tosi was a rare individual who had been allowed to go into Wounded Knee during the siege as part of a medical team with his PA trainee and AIM member George Whirlwind Soldier. At that time, AIM had taken over the tribal police in Rosebud as well as at Wounded Knee. Dr. Tosi vividly recalls a harrowing incident involving his wife Terry, one of Rosebud's two public health nurses, in her late twenties. As he tells it:

"Terry was a visiting nurse and had left to do her home visits in April of 1973. During that time, there were a lot of AIM supporters in Leonard Crow Dog's camp in Rosebud. They had been taking some hostages, probably to prepare for a prisoner swap in case the AIM warriors in Wounded Knee were captured. In any event, I became concerned when Terry did not return home from work. Someone suggested that maybe she had been kidnapped and held hostage. We were all aware that there were many AIM sympathizers on the reservation at that time and we knew that they had confiscated some cars and campers belonging to people traveling across South Dakota, so I believed the possibility of a kidnapping. I was pretty scared, but I got in my Ford Bronco and drove down to Crow Dog's camp and drove right in. There were a lot of Lakota men there but when I got out of the car, fortunately one of the Indians from Rosebud recognized me and was nice to me. I don't know his name. It was not Leonard Crow Dog. I told this person that I had reason to believe that they may have taken my wife hostage. He said they never would have done that if they knew she was my wife. He took me over to a shack and there were a few *wasichus* (whites) in the shack and standing outside. AIM warriors were watching them. I saw Terry and they let me take her. The Indian who had greeted me walked us to the car. I was totally scared because they looked pretty hostile, but I just kept my head down as we got in the car and drove away. I don't know how many hostages they had because I never went into the shack. Terry was standing outside with probably another 5 or 6 men and women. I think that they were all ultimately released without harm."

Another AIM incident happened in Rosebud Hospital's outpatient department. The area was so dilapidated and depressing that when Dr. Tosi's father came to visit and saw the poor conditions, he went home to raise money for supplies, including medical equipment, eye glasses, and TVs for patients to watch the one available TV station. He was so appalled at the condition of the worn-out floor in the outpatient department that he sent a rug to at least cover it. When the new rug was installed, it apparently didn't meet government regulations, so the administration was told to remove it. George Whirlwind Soldier called to report the problem to his AIM buddies. They all came and stood on the rug, so it couldn't be removed, and the rug stayed.

Back to the fateful day of the shooting. The medical-surgical unit had been very busy even before the Bellecourt incident, with several aides not showing up for work that day. A woman had been badly beaten at the big powwow the night before and was requiring a lot of attention. I had been caring for a young man over several days who had chest tubes, a tracheostomy (breathing tube), IVs and other supports. Despite all this, he was alert, and made it known to me that he wanted to go to the powwow too! I was impressed with the toughness of these people. I was also assigned to an older blind man who had just lost much of his leg. The hospital had no physical therapy services. I was trying to teach him to use a walker before he went home, since with no rehab available anywhere in the community there would be no professional help once he was sent home.

Luckily, Mr. Arnold, our newly-hired Assistant Director of Nurses had been working hard to mentor new graduates and to try to mold us into a capable staff. Tall and thin, with wavy sandy hair and kind blue eyes, his slow drawl had a calming effect in most situations. The good news was that we had just gotten the very first three heart monitors for the hospital, and Mr. Arnold had started showing us how to use them. The bad news was that one had a picture but no sound, and another had sound but no picture. We had little clue what any of it meant, except that of course we could recognize a flat line. If we heard an alarm, we couldn't tell which patient it was for or what was wrong. Maybe one monitor, if any, could print out an EKG strip. Besides the poor quality of these machines, we had no place to put them and so they were parked down by the maternity beds, a "nice restful" place for our sickest patients.

The medical student we'd met that first day, Lucy Reifel, had sent Dr. Tosi a patient who needed to get his heart rhythm normalized. This involved mild sedation before applying the paddles to give him a jolt of electricity. After the procedure, this patient would chant whenever Dr. Tosi would come in. When he was discharged from the hospital, he told everyone how he felt so much better, and his friends would come in wanting a "thunderbolt" too.

During the mayhem of the crowded hallway, we found a young woman hiding in the nurses' bathroom. She was two months pregnant and had been beaten by her husband who belonged to the large AIM group in the hallway, and so his wife was hiding from him. She was later admitted to the busy maternity area. Several babies were born that bustling day. It was 110 degrees outside, and I'm surprised we didn't have more heat-related incidents with the big powwow.

Down in the emergency room before the shooting victim, Clyde Bellecourt, had come upstairs to us, Dr. Tosi had been trying to start an IV. But Russell Means stopped him, saying, "You're not touching him." Leonard Crow Dog had been working on him too, as AIM's official spiritual healer and holy man, chanting and performing Lakota medicine rituals. Nonetheless, the AIM group had brought him to the hospital, apparently seeking both traditions of care, and his condition was deteriorating. He needed blood, and as the hospital had no blood bank, the usual source was tapped: the "drunk tank" at the local jail. That leads me now to wonder about the quality of the blood that we were giving our patients, with the alcohol additives, though I was unaware of this at the time. Manley Night Pipe was the tribal judge who was contacted by the docs for arrangements.

Meanwhile, Judy witnessed the operative permit that Russell Means signed for Clyde Bellecourt, and she was helping to prep him for surgery, as it was her first time working in the operating room. On the day of the shooting, Clyde Bellecourt was in the good care of an experienced local nurse, Lucille Morton, a rancher's matronly wife who knew when to be firm and when to give tender loving care. She was great at controlling the AIM guys in order to care for her patient. I'm also very pleased to report that the hospital administration wisely decided to send him out to a better equipped hospital. It was a brilliant way to defuse the tense situation for all of us. Mr. Bellecourt survived the ordeal and has spent most of his life continuing to advocate for improvements in the lives of his fellow Native Americans.

Oh, I guess I could mention that this shooting happened the day before I got my first paycheck, and I was still waiting to hear whether I'd passed my nursing boards.

Icicupi.

8. Wounded Knee, Pine Ridge Reservation.

9. Wounded Knee memorial stone with prayer ribbon ties on the fence behind.

4. Transport and the Zipper Lady

RAVERY. *WOOHITKE (WO-OH-HEE-TEE-KEH)*. HAVING OR SHOWING COURAGE.

We called her the Zipper Lady. The nurse from St. Anthony's Flying Service reminded us of the*" Cherry Ames, Flight Nurse"* book we had read as young girls. In her 30s, with brown hair pulled back oh so neatly, she wore a blue jumpsuit with a zillion zippers for all her snazzy high-tech equipment and doodads. Larger than life, a superhero to us, she carried on efficiently as she prepared the sickest patients to be airlifted to a proper medical center in Rapid City, South Dakota, Lincoln, Nebraska, or sometimes Denver, Colorado. We Rosebud staff members would gather with our noses pressed against the nursery window, enthralled as she deftly whisked a baby off to the waiting plane. The only surprise was that it didn't happen more often, as we were pitifully understaffed, undertrained, and undersupplied. The Zipper Lady's appearance always seemed to save the day. We did our best with what we had, but like the rest of the reservation, our resources were meager at best.

As a newly budding nurse, I had decided that I would never do something to a patient that I hadn't experienced myself. Shortly after I had devised that great idea, I received a doctor's order to pass an NG tube, which was about 1/4" diameter going up one's nose, down the throat and into the stomach. I understood why that patient needed this procedure and I did not, and thus ended that naive resolution.

Another principle we'd learned in nursing school was to use "nursing measures" before giving sleep medication, if possible, to avoid unwanted side effects of the meds. Sometimes repositioning or adjusting the pillow could solve the problem, though we discovered that it worked more often in books than in practice. Often a combination of nursing and meds worked best. About ten o'clock one night, the man at the end of the hall asked for a sleeping pill. Following the nursing theory I had learned in school, I first went to his room without the pill and offered him a backrub to relax him, which was then standard practice on the evening shift. He gladly accepted the backrub, but moments after I started, I felt his hands rubbing MY backside, so I quickly got him his dose of chloral hydrate to knock him out for the night, standing at an arm's length away to hand it to him with a glass of water. After that, he got all of his meds regularly from me, administered from a distance, minus the backrubs.

Mr. Arnold was our dear Assistant Director of Nurses, our mentor and champion. He took full advantage of any lull in the action to teach us about anything and everything. We had so much to learn! When we'd complain about feeling uncomfortable in a situation, he would say, "A nurse is a nurse and can function anywhere." We'd reply that we weren't really nurses yet, still waiting to hear whether or not we'd passed our nursing board exams. I clearly remember starting my first IV. I was mortified that the patient was an alert attractive young man, about my age. "Oh, why couldn't it be a sleepy old person?" I lamented. Mr. A. replied that he chose this guy because of his good veins, so it would be easier for me. Physically easier, probably, but the guy's mocking sassy attitude over my trepidation made me even more nervous. Fortunately for both of us, I did hit his vein on the first try and got the IV started.

Then there was the CVP, central venous pressure. For really sick patients, it's not enough to check their blood pressure in their arm, but there would be an IV line going into the main vein to the heart – all measurements that are automated in today's ICU. In that time, we had only a glass tube contraption almost two feet tall with teeny markings. We had to attach this tube to the central IV line, then rest the tube by the patient's chest, and try to line it up vertically by eyeballing it with the door frame to get it perpendicular for a supposedly accurate measurement. That was pretty much state of the art for the time.

After about two weeks on the job, I was given the medication room keys and assigned to pass meds for the 25 patients on the unit. We had a pharmacy, but medicines back then came in big stock bottles shared by all patients on the unit. We had little two- inch handwritten cards for each med for each patient, teeny ruffled paper cups in which to pour the pills, plastic cups for the liquid doses, and a tray with a slot for the cards by the hole for the cup. We had to triple check each patient's name, med, and dose as we poured the pills. It took me a couple of hours to painstakingly organize all these doses, with interruptions for giving pain meds in between. I also had to test the urine of all the diabetic patients before breakfast and lunch, which involved counting drops of urine into a test tube, dropping a Clinitest tablet into the urine, timing the reaction, and comparing the color to a chart. This would determine the dose of insulin for some of these patients. This also was state of the art, long before personal blood glucose testing. Diabetes incidence here then was 3.7 times the national rate, per Rosebud tribal statistics.

I finally walked out of the med room into the hall with my tray of meds all organized. However, Vonnie our beloved unit clerk had set up a fan for the 107-degree August day, and there went all my little med cards flying across the hall. Morning meds were a bit late that day, despite my best efforts.

For the patients that we were unable to save, the hospital did have a morgue. It was in the creepy basement of our condemned and, some said, haunted building. We would bathe, wrap and tag the body, and wheel it down to the basement. There were two cooler doors with rolling trays, each to accommodate one body. However, due to the remoteness of the location, lack of phones and transportation, there might be delays in locating the next of kin, or in making funeral arrangements, so there were times when we had to double up the bodies on the slabs. Nice.

We also frequently had overcrowding with the live patients. Often the rooms were all full and patients were admitted to beds in the hallways. Tuberculosis was rampant, roughly eight times the national rate, and many of the patients in the hall beds should have been on isolation precautions, had the resources only been available. We gave TB skin tests to all patients as they were admitted to test their exposure. But they often didn't stay the two to three days necessary to read the outcome of the test, so there was no record of it being positive (or negative). They probably all wondered why their arms were swollen and itchy when they went home. If a patient had been previously exposed to TB and had had prior skin tests, the reaction caused the injection site to redden, swell and itch even more with each skin test. Not only did patients have the discomfort of an irritated arm, but many went with undiagnosed and untreated active tuberculosis in the lungs, as well as advanced complications in the brain, spine, bones, and kidneys. The public health staff of two nurses was too small and homes were too remote to follow up on the test results. Even if we had told the patients who left before the test was read to contact us if their arm reacted, they likely would not have found a phone or a ride for something so minor as an irritated arm.

In a remote land with only a few phones and cars, coming to the hospital was a major ordeal for most.

Eventually a hospital administrator had the brilliant idea to put a cap on the hospital census, so that when the beds in the rooms were full, we could no longer admit more patients to the hall. At least then everyone was in a room with some privacy and sanitation. I suppose that those who would have been admitted to the hall beds were either sent home or to another hospital, at least fifty miles away. Some of our patients were discharged earlier to make room for sicker folks coming in.

Sometimes we had to transport patients that weren't deemed sick enough to warrant the cost of the specialized Zipper Lady. Besides transporting Quannah Crow Dog on my first day of work, weeks later I was assigned to accompany a 14- year-old girl who was about 6 months pregnant with twins and in labor as she was airlifted to Denver. I monitored her vital signs and contractions and tried to keep her calm. But again, my main strategy was prayer. I really had no equipment or expertise to handle the situation if she should deliver two premature babies during the flight. I felt I was in way over my head, as usual. We did get her to Denver safely, but a couple of days later they sent her back to Rosebud, saying it had been false labor! I never heard what happened to her after that, though I wondered from time to time. Did she get sent out again? Did she give up on the hospital and deliver at home with a midwife or a medicine man? How did her babies do? I didn't see her in the hospital on any of my shifts.

Rosemarie had her own excitement transporting a pregnant woman. As she tells it, "The doctor suspected the young mother was in early stages of labor with a pending breech delivery. He thought there was enough time to fly her to Rapid City for delivery and asked me to be the escort. Just before leaving the emergency room for the airstrip, the doctor asked if I had ever delivered a baby by breech. Of course, I hadn't! So, he gave me a thirty second lesson on breech delivery along with the emergency delivery kit and wished me good luck. The delivery kit was pretty basic, consisting of a basin, two towels, two umbilical clamps, sterile scissors, some gloves, and a baby blanket. But then, I thought maybe that's all that was needed. At the air strip I told the pilots that I wanted the patient's stretcher positioned in the plane with her head lower than her hips; I didn't want any pressure on her cervix. Thankfully a few hours later we arrived at Rapid City hospital with the mother still pregnant. I'm glad I didn't have to find out if I'd needed additional items in the delivery kit!"

The delivery kit was never offered to me on my transport, though I doubt it would have made a substantial difference with premature twins. I'm sure the Zipper Lady would have had a perfectly stocked delivery kit and skills to match.

Rosemarie relates another episode about a year later, in late summer of 1974: "I had just gotten off the night shift and was looking forward to my day off. Of course, this meant that I was up for ambulance or flight escort if needed. In the late morning my phone rang and, sure enough, I was told that I was needed for an escort. The patient, in stable condition, was a high-ranking officer of AIM who had been shot by a state policeman. I was further told that FBI men were hiding in the hills surrounding the hospital, aiming their guns at the Indians who had surrounded the hospital with rifles in hand. The supervisor ended the call by telling me, 'Just walk in through the hospital doors like you know what you're doing.' I helped prepare the patient for transport and soon it was time to leave the hospital. I climbed inside through the back of the ambulance and took my position next to the patient. All along the ten-mile ride to the Mission air strip, Indians had lined the route, standing with their fists in the air just like in the Billy Jack movie. That was the longest ten-mile ride I ever had."

Sonny Waln was our usual ambulance driver, and we would give him money to bring back food for us from the McDonald's in Rapid City, about five hours away. Of course, by the time we got it, the food was cold and the fries were soggy but it still tasted good to us, and as Dr. Tosi said, "It was exciting to spend money on something." Sonny wasn't always our driver though, and we had some other real doozies.

Stephanie was another young newly- graduated nurse from Maryland, who had arrived in Rosebud a few weeks before us. She was tall and distinguished by her remarkable curly chestnut- brown hair, freckles, nervous energy, and hearty laugh. She had arranged for a couple of days off after having her four wisdom teeth pulled. Alas, she had not arranged to leave town to recuperate. She got a desperate call begging her go on an ambulance run to take a man with internal injuries from a drunk driving accident to the Rapid City Hospital, 350 miles round trip. She tried to decline, but of course there was nobody else who could go. The man needed surgery, but Rosebud's surgeon was not available. Steph recalls this story:

"We'd already had to stop once at a local hospital along the way to restart the IV that the patient had pulled out while thrashing around the back of the ambulance. He had required sedation, which needed a doctor's order. The ambulance had then gotten a couple of hours beyond Rosebud when the driver said he had to pull over and take a nap! I looked at him like he had two heads and said, "You can't do that! We have to get this patient there in a hurry!" The driver replied that he was hung over and really could not stay awake and proceeded to park at the side of the road and pass out. We were in the middle of nowhere in the middle of the night. I still had chipmunk cheeks from the wisdom teeth extractions and cotton packing. I shoved the driver into the passenger seat, hopped into the driver's seat, and drove off to Rapid City at 80 mph, as there were no speed limits. I was driving with my left hand, looking back to check the IV, and to swat with my right hand at the patient, who was also drunk but thrashing around again, and to yell for him to lie back down! As we were approaching Rapid City, I had to wake up the driver to find the hospital, plus I was concerned that a special drivers' license might be required to drive the ambulance. Several hours later we returned from that wild ride and I went thankfully back to my own sick bed."

We all took our turns transporting patients, and Judy had the most memorable flight as part of her orientation. She was assigned to bring an older woman named Mable back from Omaha, Nebraska where she'd been treated after suffering a stroke in Rosebud. As Judy tells it:

"The patient had reached maximum function and needed to come home. Well how exciting. Air transport. Wow. Yeah, well I'd heard some stories and thought I was braced for the challenge ... First of all, arriving at the take-off point I saw the small single engine plane on a strip of asphalt that ended in the town dump. But I got into the two-seater and off we went. The pilot was very quiet on the trip, so I didn't learn much about this Antelope Air Service. We landed in Omaha about 3 p.m. It was immediately obvious that Mabel was not there and ready for transport. This annoyed the pilot, so he called to find out where she was. As time passed and no Mabel, he began to pace and look at his watch. His increasing anxiety was very noticeable. Then finally Mabel arrived on a stretcher. She was loaded into the back of the plane, with her head between the pilot's seat and mine. She was unable to talk. I checked vital signs and off we went heading west, back to Rosebud, in total silence with a very tense pilot. Finally, I couldn't take it any longer and asked what the problem was. I probably shouldn't have asked, because the answer wasn't something I wanted to hear. Daylight was fading and there was only one light on the plane. On top of that, there were no lights at the landing site! Now there were two anxious people flying west in silence. Since the Mission airfield was secluded by the dump, the blue bulbs were regularly shot out, and now were not being replaced! As the world faded to dark, the little plane continued heading west until all of a sudden, the pilot broke his silence and said, "I think we're here." Well exactly where was "here"? No lights. Anywhere. And suddenly, "Hold on," and down we dived. The sudden dive had me bracing for a crash, and then we were heading back up. Level off. Check Mabel. And now we were well aware of what she had had for supper. Mixed vegetables, all back in full view, and I was sweeping her mouth to try and prevent her from aspirating the food into her lungs. Just as I thought we had stabilized, down we went again. No crash, and up again. Talk about a roller coaster without a track, as the pilot continued his search in the dark for the runway. And then it happened. Two headlights from a truck went on below us. That's it! Our landing site! And down we went again. Never was there such a welcome feeling than bumpy bump bump as we rolled along the ground, then stopped. The plane had missed the runway and made a bumpy but safe landing in a field. Thank you, God! However, the ambulance was not there to bring the patient the last ten miles to the hospital. The guys asked me if I wanted to wait, and I said, "No Way! We're not waiting!" They brought Mable and me the final distance to the hospital in the back of a station wagon. We'd survived my nursing orientation."

Another triumph of Rosebud ingenuity over desperation. And all without the Zipper Lady's nifty gadgets. We'd all been thrown into the deep end and somehow managed the challenges, so far.

Woohitike.

5. The hill

RESPECT. *WAWOOHOLA (WAH-WO-O-HO-LAH)*. TO BE CONSIDERATE, TO HOLD IN HIGH ESTEEM.

Growing up in Connecticut, I loved going barefoot in the soft cool green grass of our suburban lawn. One warm early fall day in Rosebud, feeling far from home, I took off my shoes to climb the hill behind the hospital. I aimed for the cemetery on top where the Brule Sioux Chief Spotted Tail was buried under a large metal cross.

In 1861 the Brule people had chosen Spotted Tail to lead in them in the battles against the U.S. Army to save their land and traditions. Spotted Tail made several trips to Washington, D.C. where he saw the masses of people and power. He knew that Indians would be outnumbered and outgunned in battles. He made the tough decision to cooperate and work toward peace rather than see his people overrun and killed, becoming a peacemaker in a difficult time. Their sacred Black Hills, along with other land was later lost to the U.S. government. Spotted Tail's cousin, Crow Dog killed him in 1891, feeling that Spotted Tail had shamed his people.

According to Leonard Crow Dog in his book *Crow Dog*, there were other factors in a running feud between these cousins. While the Lakota considered killing enemies a brave deed, killing a fellow tribe member was the worst offense. As Spotted Tail's family prepared his body for his funeral, Crow Dog went to pray and purify himself. Spotted Tail's family raised his body onto a scaffold in the traditional way, but the white authorities said he must be buried, so the grave on the hill was established. Crow Dog and his friends tried to make peace. He paid money, horses and blankets to Spotted Tail's family, settling in the Indian way. The Brule elders then exiled Crow Dog and four generations of his family from Rosebud in 1891. But the authorities were not satisfied with this arrangement. Many whites felt that he had gotten away with murder. They took Crow Dog to trial and sentenced him to be hanged. However, he won his appeal, with the decision that the government has no jurisdiction on the reservation in tribal matters. Crow Dog was the first Indian to win a case before the U.S. Supreme Court. Many members of both the Crow Dog and Spotted Tail families, among others, lie together in that cemetery atop the hill overlooking Rosebud.

By Lakota tradition, guilt lasts for four generations. Leonard Crow Dog is the fourth generation, the great-grandson. He still lives outside of town. Despite the belligerent personality that we saw, Leonard Crow Dog was a spiritual medicine man who hosted many ceremonies on his land at Crow Dog's Paradise, in the White River valley beyond Rosebud's hill. He was instrumental in the revival of the then-outlawed Lakota rituals and culture. We would quickly drive past his house on our way to the lake, seeing the framework of the sweat lodge for purification and the pole for the grueling and sacred sun dance of sacrifice and prayer. It was always held in early August to honor the anniversary of Spotted Tail's death. Honor is another key cultural value. The sun dance is where men pierced their chest and back muscles with sharp wood, tying thongs to drag along buffalo skulls. While fasting and dancing around the pole their eyes and bodies followed the sun across the sky for three days, or until their skin and muscles tore open. Several of our patients had these chest scars from a sun dance ceremony. We felt fear and respect as we tried to catch a glimpse of the legendary Crow Dog whenever we sped by his Paradise. But in his book, *Crow Dog*, he states on page 39, "In 1991 Chief Spotted Tail came to Crow Dog's sun dance. He wore his war bonnet. He pierced. He hung from the tree. I prayed together with him. I fanned him with my eagle wing. So now we are friends. The bad feeling is gone. It's over."

I was joined on the hill by the communal dog Blue, a sweet black mongrel with soft curly fur, who got passed around, claimed by a parade of owners as Public Health Service personnel came and left the compound. I'd always wanted a dog, so I was thrilled to claim Blue as mine when I realized he didn't have another current owner. We stopped to sit and rest halfway up the steep hill. We paused partly to catch my breath, and partly because though my feet were tough, the grass was tougher here—very coarse and rough, and I was too lazy to go back down and get my shoes. I wanted a place to collect my thoughts, as lately we had been so busy at the hospital I hadn't had time to process the recent events.

First, it was shigella season at Rosebud, a form of dysentery that can be deadly for the young and old. A major cause is inadequate sanitation. The pediatric wing was full of babies inflicted with severe green diarrhea, and a typical day was spent changing endless diapers in the large ward room of 12 to 15 babies. Checking and restarting the IVs in their fragile scalp veins, filling bottles, washing hands between every encounter, we just tried to keep these tiny patients alive while the bacteria was shredding the lining of their guts. All day long, or all night long we bustled to care for these little ones. When we finished one lap around the room it was time to start another. We gave them diluted Jell-O water in their bottles just to get them to drink anything at all. The hall on the medical floor was lined with 4-6 extra stretchers with older patients suffering in the throes of shigella dysentery, with absolutely no privacy. We changed bedpans and sheets as fast as possible. Even in 2004, the incidence of shigella dysentery at Rosebud was still four times the national rate (according to Oski's *Essential Pediatrics*, p. 289). The smell went home and stayed with us, even after a shower. I'd never even heard of shigella before. Many of the kids also had impetigo, a skin infection often associated with squalor. Those times remain much too clearly in our memories.

Later, on the medical-surgical side, one rollicking night Judy and I, along with our wonderful aide Lorna Her Many Horses were caring for thirty patients. We had fifteen IVs to watch (before automated pumps), and a woman whose childbirth labor also demanded my attention. These women were so stoic they often received no pain meds for childbirth, and their lack of expression in labor could make it hard to assess their progress. Then Dr. Tosi called Judy to come down and help in the ER with a severely injured patient, which left Lorna and I to cover the entire floor and the woman in labor. Later, I called Dr. Tosi in the ER, to tell him that the woman was getting close to delivery. He said he'd try to come up soon. The delivery was imminent and still no doc. Nobody to catch the baby but me. All I could think of was the quote by Hattie McDaniel who played Mammy in *Gone with the Wind*, "Miz Scarlett, I don't know nuthin bout birthin no babies!" I had been present at deliveries in school, but certainly wasn't trained to perform one. No matter, the baby was coming anyway. I took Lorna, our calm and experienced nurses' aide to help me, and borrowed the LPN from pediatrics to watch the other 30 patients on the crowded unit. We got the mom into the delivery room, prepped her, and still no doc. I put on the gloves, prayed, and caught the baby. He cried right away and seemed healthy, thank goodness. It's always a privilege to witness the miracle of a new life coming into the world. I frequently am moved to tears in the delivery room, and that night was no exception, but this time the tears were not only of awe, but also immense relief and exhaustion.

After the birth, everybody was relatively fine on the unit, except that all of my IVs had run dry because the LPN wasn't licensed to tend to IVs, and after the birth I had to restart all fifteen (no IV team—just us). This was before we had machines to monitor the flow and to beep when there was a problem. We had to put a tape on the side of the glass IV solution bottle and calculate how fast the liter should flow in, marking the times on the tape. Then we had to calculate the drops per minute, and then count the drops with our watch and adjust the flow valve to get the proper rate. If the metal needle moved within the vein, or out of the vein, the flow could change quickly, so the IVs required frequent checking. If the fluid flowed in too fast, it could cause the heart to overload and a fragile patient could die. If the IV stopped, a clot could form with potential to break off and cause a heart attack or stroke. Often there were medications added to the IVs, which made the monitoring even more critical. Once when Lorna's son was in with an IV she refused to leave his side, sitting vigil to watch his IV.

At 3 a.m. I got a call from Judy that I was to admit the patient that they had been working on for several hours in the ER. The man was so severely beaten that it was hard to recognize a face in the bruised pulp. He was unconscious, alternating with combative delirium, and he needed very close attention. Anyplace else, he would have been in an Intensive Care Unit, but Rosebud's ICU was still on the drawing board, so we did it all. Dr. Tosi even had to take all the X-rays himself that night. As it turned out, when the Intensive Care room was finally organized and equipped with monitors, we were given a brief training and we had to staff it ourselves anyway. Judy didn't come back to us when the battered patient came to our floor because people kept coming to the ER with injuries. Finally, at 5 a.m. she returned to help us on the medical unit, after having had lessons in how to take x-rays and how to suture. What a night! The next night I saw the new mom walking in the hall, and she asked calmly, if not a little too sweetly if I was going to deliver another baby that night. Hah! It was good to see her up walking though, and with a healthy baby. After nights like that, we would go to our assistant director of nurses, our champion, Mr. Arnold, to report how desperately we needed more help. He would typically reply, "Did anyone die? No? Then you did just fine!" Just about a month had passed since I'd been notified that I'd passed my nursing boards and was a real RN, I thought as I sat on the hill.

With all these things happening, we looked for anything to make us laugh and smile. Along came Halloween. We went searching to buy pumpkins and decorations, including Charlie Brown's Great Pumpkin book of Halloween carols. What fun we had one night with our wonderful sweet LPN Julie Emory and her kids, and Ron Arnold and his kids dressing up and eating treats. We spread newspaper on the kitchen floor for the pumpkin carving, savoring the distinctive smell of the bright stringy innards. We separated the seeds from the orange slime to roast in the oven, adding a little salt for a tasty snack. Lighting candles in our finished artwork, we opened the Great Pumpkin book and sang Halloween songs together.

Then there was the lawyer, just a little older than we were, who offered his "studly" services to the lonely and socially deprived community. He was a frequent flier in the outpatient department, coming in regularly for hefty double barrel penicillin shots in each backside cheek to treat recurrent gonorrhea infections. Gonorrhea here is even now more than four times the national average, according to the Rosebud STD clinic. Amazingly, a couple of years later, I met him while crossing a busy street in New York City. He called to me, smiling, and seeing his familiar face was a pleasant surprise in NYC. Later, after shaking the hand he'd offered me I was still glad to wash my hands.

Speaking of STDs, a group of doctors had decided to test a large dark-colored stray dog named Thor for gonorrhea. Perhaps they had noticed some symptoms and were concerned for their own dogs' health. With no veterinary services in Rosebud, they took it upon themselves to obtain a sample from the dog. But when they tried to send it in for testing, they realized that a patient's last name was required. So, they completed the paperwork identifying the patient as Thor Dark Dog. The test came back positive, and an agent came from the state health department in Pierre, finding and questioning the real Dark Dog family (name changed) about contacts. The family was outraged and puzzled as to how this had happened. The docs were surprised and chagrinned that there was an actual family named Dark Dog.

Meanwhile, my friend Judy who had brought me to Rosebud, had told me that her fiancé Russell was coming at Christmas. For multiple reasons, she was considering returning back East with him in January. This was a blow to me, as I would miss her terribly. Also, it meant I would have to get a car of my own, as there was no public transit and we were miles from anywhere. We decided to drive to the nearest car dealership in Winner, South Dakota, 50 miles away. I ordered a new Chevy Nova, in a metallic green color that called to me. It was only later that I realized why the color was so familiar, and so I called the car Shigella.

We occasionally collaborated with a few local medicine men, traditional spiritual healers. John Fire was a healer also known as Lame Deer. Dr. Tosi tells how they delivered some babies together, with John Fire chanting and dancing, once helping to turn a breech baby around for an easier birth. They got to know and trust each other, so that when John Fire became anemic and needed B12 shots, he would sneak into Dr. Tosi's kitchen for a shot so local folks wouldn't know he needed the white medicine. Another time a little girl about 10 years old was brought in to the hospital having frequent seizures. Despite trying several medications, the seizures continued, so her family brought a medicine man to the hospital to try his healing powers. This too brought little immediate improvement, and the family took the girl home under the medicine man's care. I never learned what happened to her.

I sat on the hill running my fingers through Blue's soft curls and savoring the sweet smell of the dry grass and sage. The sunlight was so bright that the grass shimmered and it backlit the small hairs on the plant seeds. I felt a heightened sense of existence, really feeling a part of the scene and could begin to appreciate the Indian ritual of sitting for a vision quest on this hill near Chief Spotted Tail's grave.

Contemplating my place in life, I noticed a tall portly man walking slowly and unevenly in the distance, carrying a stick and a large sack as he looked down. He seemed absorbed in whatever he was doing, roaming in my direction. As he approached, I recognized him as the hospital lab tech who'd had polio and wore leg braces.

When he was close enough, I said, "Hi, Ray. What are you doing?"

He replied, "You shouldn't be sittin up here on the hill. I'm huntin rattlesnakes and I've caught quite a few already!"

I could now see the sizeable canvas sack was wiggling. I quickly scrambled up, and he carefully walked me back down the hill to my shoes, on the lookout for more snakes on the way. I asked, "What do you do with the snakes? "

He said proudly, "I use 'em to make things. If ya wanna see, ya can come over to my place in a little bit when I'm done huntin the rattlers here." He told me where he lived in the hospital compound on Pill Hill.

I went to find Judy to come with me to his house for his interesting tour. His projects were pretty unique, and not just a little creepy. His freezer contained several rattlesnakes of various sizes. He chilled the snakes to get them semi-stiff so he could fashion them into various "artistic" positions. Depending on the size of the snakes, he would mold them into an acrylic- type of form. Then he could make anything from refrigerator magnets and belt buckles with baby snakes, to coffee table tops with the biggest ones! He had rings made from the snake heads with fangs and beady eyes. I've never seen anything like it since. I didn't think to ask where he sold them, long before the internet and miles from anywhere. They were definitely not something I was tempted to own or give as a gift.

The multitude of rattlesnakes did not escape local kids' attention either. Judy recalls one middle school boy coming to the ER with a nasty rattlesnake bite on his swollen hand after playing catch with the snake. The boys would also hide one of those rattlers in high school lockers, bringing us more snakebite victims.

10. Crow Dog's compound entrance outside Rosebud.

I'm not sure my solitude and contemplation on the hill that day did much to help me find respite from the frenzy. But I do know that I didn't go back there to sit and think again, nor did I savor the dubious joys of going barefoot again in Rosebud. The hill with the cemetery was peaceful to contemplate, but it held its own dangers, so typical of the complexity of Rosebud then and now.

Wawoohola.

11. Spotted Tail's grave.

12. Graveyard on the hill.

6. Thanksgiving

HONOR. *WAYUONIHAN (WAH-YOU-O-KNEE-HAN).* TO HAVE INTEGRITY, TO HAVE AN HONEST AND UPRIGHT CHARACTER.

"I wish I could see what's out there," Mom said, peering through the car window.

"There's nothing to see," I replied as my brother Rick drove on into the 100-mile stretch of darkness between the Pierre airport and Rosebud. My small family had come to spend Thanksgiving with me. All three of us now together again, as my dad had died when I was seven and my brother was ten. This was the first time I wouldn't be home to celebrate the holidays with them in Connecticut. They had flown in earlier that afternoon, but my brand-new car, Shigella broke down as we were leaving Pierre. Unfortunately, we had to be towed back to town. The friendly mechanic had asked where we headed, but like many locals, he became cold and hostile when I told him that I was working at the Indian hospital in Rosebud. He spoke of "wild Injuns, gun-toting rebels and radicals," referring mainly to the recent Wounded Knee uprising with AIM and the FBI shooting. His words stung me. But we seemed to be at the mercy of this man as we remained stranded with our dead car. My brother reminded me that I won a smile from the mechanic, though, when I gave him a bottle of wine for his prompt emergency attention. Luckily it was a minor fix that delayed us only a few hours, so now we were back on the road travelling in the dark.

Meanwhile, although my family's arrival was relatively easy, Judy's sister Merrilyn wasn't so lucky. Snow comes early and fast to South Dakota, with drifts commonly up to ten feet, as we would learn. The next day's snow diverted Merrilyn's flight to Denver, and then back to Pierre. Judy had gone to Pierre to pick up Merrilyn and had brought Stephanie along, so they looked for lodging since Merrilyn wouldn't arrive until the morning. They found the Paradise Motel but were firmly told to use only one bed and not to dirty the sheets on the second bed in the room! Merrilyn made the trek to Rosebud, wondering where the heck she had landed. The rolling desolate landscape was a far cry from her busy Cornell University campus in Ithaca, New York, but she was inquisitive and so joined our family to try and figure out what we were doing in Rosebud.

Ever since we'd arrived in Rosebud we'd known the seasons would change from the baking summer heat into fall. We knew we would miss the beautiful scarlets, oranges, golds, limes and rich combinations of fall colors from our New England home. But we had been assured that we would be wowed by the beauty of the aspens when they changed color. The prairie is not known for its abundance of trees. We watched the green quaking leaves of the few aspen turn one shade of yellow and then fall off. The burned grass of summer turned a deader brown, and Smoky the Bear signs said "Only You Can Prevent Prairie Fires," not "Forest Fires" like I'd always seen back home. My appreciation of nature had yet to fully mature, and the wide-open plains had revealed to me only a few of its most obvious treasures: buffalo, prairie dogs, and vast sunsets. My New England mindset perceived the open land as empty, unable to fully appreciate its own vast but stark beauty and more subtle treasures.

The next day as my mom looked out into the light of her first morning, she said, "You're right, there's nothing here." Despite the fact that we had recently moved from our trailer in Mission into a two-bedroom brick apartment in government housing next to the hospital on "Pill Hill," the view was simply of rolling grassland and sage prairie with big sky and very few trees. The tiny general store, post office, tribal offices and brand new Sinte Gleska Community College in the center of Rosebud were over the hill and out of sight. We routinely drove fifty miles each way weekly for groceries, supplies, and to the nearest traffic light in Valentine, Nebraska.

Our apartment had generously sized rooms and appeared to be of a similar vintage as the hospital. Two additional units in the building housed other nurses. They told us our new home was said to be haunted as it was built on an Indian burial ground, but we never heard from those unfortunate neighbors. I liked the kitchen's yellowing cabinets with retro latches and older but functional appliances. The aromas of aging wood and paint mingled with ghosts of past meals. Unlike our recent trailer home, these solid floors did not shake as we walked through, though we did hear an occasional squeak from the hardwood. The functional government furniture was comfortable, if not trendy. I don't recall having a TV, which was fine since Rosebud only received one channel. We added a few personal touches with books, photos of our loved ones, my guitar, and small travel souvenirs from our recent cross-country trip. Bit by bit, local items began to join the accumulation: an arrangement of yucca pods, Richard Fool Bull's colorful courting flute, and my beading loom with rainbow supplies of tiny beads.

At the hospital, work kept us very busy. We worked all three shifts, by rotating on day shift for two weeks, then evening shift for two weeks, and two weeks on nights, then starting over on days. This doesn't account for all the overtime and double shifts we endured. Sleep deprivation became the norm, as did facing continuous crises. With the move from Mission to Rosebud a few weeks before Thanksgiving, we could now walk the 100 yards to work and didn't have to carpool. I'm sure that made scheduling our shifts easier, with the freedom to expect us to work at any time. An advantage for us was that we could see and hear what was coming into the Emergency Room and leave the house before they could call us in to work extra hours. We'd usually escape to the Western Bowl and Café in Mission for chocolate cream pie. However, it was not unusual to get a call at midnight to come in, telling us that Montilou, the Director of Nurses, had added us to the schedule but had forgotten to tell us.

In early November, one chilly morning around four o'clock I awakened to a scream. I hopped out of bed to check on Judy, finding her standing on her bed in a pink flowered flannel nightgown, green plaid flannel shirt, and high-top brown shit-kicker boots, clutching her arms to her chest and looking terrified. She had been reading and had seen a mouse run into her closet. This was a farm girl used to getting up early and being amidst lots of nature, but I guess not when it was in her own bedroom. We had survived camping all around the country, with plagues of black flies, mosquitoes, gnats, ants and scorpions, so I was very surprised at how upset she was by a little brown field mouse. I reassured her that I'd handle this. Not wanting to risk a bite though, I bent over and took one of her shoes, using it to move the other shoes one by one out of the closet, looking for the little mouse. With the last shoe came the mouse, scurrying across her floor, crossing the hall, and into my bedroom closet. I put a towel under the door to keep it there and went back to sleep. We got some mouse traps and poison on our next grocery trip, and we didn't see the mouse running around again.

We took our family on a day trip of 200 miles to the Badlands, which resemble a stark moonscape, an exotic contrast to the family's usual Eastern woodland views. We passed our neighbors at the Pine Ridge Reservation on the way, driving by a little shack and ramshackle truck sporting a bumper sticker saying, "Custer wore Arrow Shirts." My mom, with her permed salt-and-pepper hair and brown eyes, wore a dark fake fur coat, so that when she bent over for a closer look at genuine tumbleweed and sage she resembled a buffalo. We named her Buffalo Woman. Our guests especially enjoyed seeing the prairie dogs. We included a stop at Wall Drug for buffalo burgers and their famous "free water," an inspired novelty when the store was established for the pioneers in the sun baked prairie.

Judy had insisted that I read the book, *Bury My Heart at Wounded Knee,* before we went to Rosebud. The author, Dee Brown, relates the sad and terrible history of the 1890 massacre and surrounding events, and I was saddened more to discover how the injustices were continuing as I learned more and more of this place and people whose culture was so new to me.

We showed our visitors the small but fascinating historical museum in the town of St. Francis, about ten miles away. Among the many interesting artifacts were some painted buckskin shirts from the Ghost Dancers of the 1870s - 1880s. Many had bullet holes. Here is their story (*www.native-americans-online.com*):

In 1870 a Paiute medicine man named Wovoka in Nevada had had a vision of reuniting the Native people with their ancestors' spirits. The returning spirits would fight on the Natives' behalf to eliminate the white people who had oppressed them. The Native cultures and all the buffalo would be restored, bringing peace, prosperity, and unity to all Native people throughout the region. This vision came at a time when the Native populations had been decimated, along with their hope. Years of summer drought, prairie fires, winter blizzards and bitter cold along with the massive buffalo hunts had eroded the food supply. Only half the children survived, and many people died of hopelessness. A total solar eclipse had brought thoughts of the end of the world. Into this time of despair came this new belief. Wovoka would be their Savior. A central doctrine of the vision was the special Ghost Dance, and the dance outfits painted with magical symbols were just as important as the dance itself. Original Ghost Dancers also practiced prayer and peaceful coexistence. Many other tribes travelled to Wovoka to learn the dance and join the movement. This is remarkable due to the diversity of Native languages and cultures, along with the fact that most were by then contained on reservations and not free to travel at will. Two Lakota Sioux men named Kicking

Bear and Short Bull brought the Ghost Dance with its hope to the Rosebud and Pine Ridge areas. Dancers fell down with powerful visions and brought gifts from the spiritual world, as described by Leonard Crow Dog in his book *Crow Dog*. The people began to feel empowered and some whites saw them as a threat. In addition, some Lakota may have believed that the magic symbols on the dance outfits were not only spiritual but that they would protect them from bullets. Although the Lakota were by now few in number and on reservations, their renewing energy and spirit alarmed the military and Indian agencies, leading directly to the death of Sitting Bull and to the December 1890 Massacre of hundreds at Wounded Knee in Pine Ridge.

Weeks before our guests' arrival, in anticipation of our Thanksgiving holiday, Judy and I had bought a few decorations and supplies. Closer to Thanksgiving, the family all piled back in the car to get the groceries for our holiday feast, and to see the sand hills, Fort Niobrara buffalo, and sage grass near Valentine. We picked out our turkey and fixins and had them boxed and wrapped for the hour ride home. Since we wouldn't be together for Christmas, I bought my brother Rick's gift, a gray Stetson cowboy hat, which we took turns modeling. Later I beaded a hatband for it. He got a lot of attention back in Connecticut as he squeezed his six-foot frame and that hat into his Volkswagen Superbeetle.

My mom and Merrilyn were busy organizing the food in the kitchen for the big feast. Unfortunately, when we pulled out our disposable roasting pan, we discovered that it had become the final resting place of the mouse we had been hunting a couple of weeks earlier. Since we couldn't make another two-hour round trip to the store, we disposed of the mouse and washed the pan thoroughly for the turkey. We had a paper Thanksgiving tablecloth, napkins, plates, candles, and we thought we were so fancy.

On Thanksgiving Day, Judy and I worked the day shift, so Mom and Merrilyn, who was a Home Economics teacher, did all the cooking. We invited the hospital's evening staff to come and share the festive dinner with us. The apartment smelled of turkey and pumpkin pie as we dragged our weary bodies home and got recharged with the warmth of family and comradery. A steady parade of hospital staff took turns coming over. The highlight—literally—was when two-year-old Freddy Thundershield set fire to the tablecloth by tipping over the lit candles! We learned that candles, a paper tablecloth, and a two- year-old are not a good mix. Our friend Stephanie threw her drink on the fire causing a larger flame, so her lesson was not to throw alcohol on a fire. We did quickly get the small blaze under control, but the now soggy holiday table was less fancy for the mishap. I can't remember how many people we fed, but it was a very special Thanksgiving with the First Americans and the visitors. The irony was that we were having Thanksgiving on an Indian reservation with Indians who weren't really happy with what the whites had done since 1620 in this country. However, it was a time to celebrate, so we did. Together.

Wayuonihan.

13. Fall at Rosebud.

14. Ma B: my mother as *Buffalo Woman*.

15. Mr. Arnold, Assistant Director of Nurses, with his daughter.

7. Christmas

GENEROSITY. *CANTEYUKE (CHAN-TE-YOU-KEH)*. TO GIVE, TO SHARE, TO HAVE A HEART.

It was indeed a Christmas miracle that five of us nurses were approved to have sixteen hours off at the same time. We five made up almost half the entire nursing staff of the hospital. We wanted to go Christmas shopping together in Sioux Falls. Judy and I had done a little shopping in Pierre when we'd dropped off our Thanksgiving visitors and had gotten a few gifts on our grocery runs to Valentine, but it was slim pickings. As this was before the time of the internet and personal computers, the only other option was catalog shopping. But we had to send away for the catalogs, and even had to know which catalogs to request before we could mail order anything—a cumbersome process. In our great wisdom, a 450-mile round trip visit to Sioux Falls seemed like a fine idea. Judy, Stephanie, Susan Beeson, and newly-hired Rose piled with me into my green car Shigella. To maximize our limited time off, we hit the road as soon as Judy got off of the night shift. Since she had to be back for the next night shift, we brought her breakfast to eat in the car, and she changed from her uniform into her shopping clothes in the crowded back seat between friends.

I started off our driving adventure while Judy changed. When we left the Rosebud reservation and the road became a four-lane with actual traffic, I had a mild panic attack and someone else took over. I guess I had gotten too acclimated to rural Rosebud, or I was just too tired or excited. We stopped at the nearest McDonalds in Mitchell, 200 miles from Rosebud, for a rare treat of a Big Mac and fries. The driving time passed quickly with lively conversation.

By early afternoon our carload arrived in Sioux Falls and we found a small shopping mall. However, we all had the same reaction: we didn't know which way to go or where to start! We were paralyzed with sensory overload from the crowds, lights, music, decorations, and an abundance of stores and choices. Boy, did we feel like hicks! It was an unexpected shock after months of Rosebud's desolation. We had been so excited to explore the shopping possibilities but all we could do was gawk at it all with a glazed look in our eyes. Eventually, someone broke the spell and bought something, then we all began to jump into the holiday spirit to find and buy some special gifts. We enjoyed a festive dinner and cocktails atop the rotating Holiday Inn, overlooking all of the lights of Sioux Falls. That was really a unique treat to top off a fun and successful day.

We had experienced the jolt of culture shock after just a few months in Rosebud. Imagine leaving the reservation for the first time after spending your entire life there. One might begin to sense a little insight and empathy as to one of the many reasons that actually moving away from the reservation is so difficult for many.

Driving back to Rosebud that December night, it began to rain. Then as the temperature dropped the rain gradually froze into black ice. The car careened into a spin and we skidded off the interstate into the ditch of the median, facing the opposite direction. The sudden jolt certainly woke up those who'd been napping in the back seat. Everyone was shaken but miraculously nobody was hurt. Thankfully the car was fine too, so after a few deep breaths, we got ourselves out of the ditch. Switching drivers, we continued trying to beat Judy's 11 p.m. target to start working the night shift. We reminded ourselves that this car held nearly half of the nursing staff of the hospital! Gradually the frozen rain turned to snow, blowing and drifting. As the weather worsened, we stopped to find a pay phone and Judy called the hospital to report that she would be late, if arriving at all that night.

Mr. Arnold told her, "That's ok; I'll call Nancy to come in."

Judy said. "No sir, she's with me."

"Then I'll call Stephanie."

"She's with us."

"Beeson?"

"With us."

"Rosemarie?"

"Here too."

"Ok. Well, I'll go in and see you when you get here."

"Thank you, Mr. Arnold!" And we truly meant it.

As we crossed the Missouri River the weather cleared, so Judy did make it back for work, like Cinderella, even though she arrived a little late.

December brought an emotional roller coaster with the exhaustion of overwork and homesickness, but with a few warm fuzzy times as well. Occasional well-timed letters and phone calls from friends and family cheered us from our doldrums. One evening I arrived at work to find two bare Christmas trees on the unit. Surprisingly it was a rare slow night, so we all made ornaments and decorations, and by the end of our shift it looked quite festive. Another evening I gathered a handful of folks who were off duty to go caroling through the compound of Pill Hill and through the hospital. Not the world's best performance but a sincere touch of cheer for us all.

As Christmas neared, Judy looked like an elf, dancing around the tree in her green pants and fuzzy boots. The darkened tree lot had appeared to be closed but Mr. Harney came outside, saying that he would like nothing better than to sell us a Christmas tree. Judy had forgotten her purse so I dug for change, feeling like a kid buying candy as I counted out coins. The light snow landed on the windshield, and for the first time I saw the flakes as six-sided individual crystals—how beautiful. Maybe it was worth venturing out in the minus twenty-seven-degree wind chill after all.

Stephanie came over to help us set up the fragrant tree in the corner. We took pictures to mail home, reaching out to family and friends. Longing for Christmas music but with no radio or stereo, we broke into song to accompany the festivities. As is often the case with impromptu carols, the spirit far outshined the melody. We had no real decorations, so we tied pine cones with red ribbons and added bows to the tree. After our next weekly trip to Valentine, Nebraska, a few plastic snowflakes joined the sparse decor. It was beautiful in a Charlie Brownish way. Our first Christmas away from home inspired our determination to make it as good as we possibly could.

On Christmas morning, I arrived home from working the night shift to find Judy asleep under our decorated tree, waiting for me. We had each received several big boxes of gifts from family, and it looked like a sea of presents beneath our tree. After we opened them, we felt overwhelmed by our excess in a land of so little. We just had to share, so we re-wrapped several of our gifts to distribute to those we knew who had not received much, if any. That felt much more appropriate to us in Rosebud.

There were only two little children, about three years old, on the pediatric ward. Donald and Belinda weren't sick but had been dropped off for babysitting by their parents and abandoned for the holiday. While most Lakota children are loved and treasured, we learned that sometimes parents bundled and warmed up kids to raise their temperature so they would seem sick and be admitted. When the symptoms resolved sometimes these parents were unavailable for days to come and reclaim their children. Amazingly, one of the moms had won $20,000 in a lawsuit against the tribe and she'd apparently wanted the freedom to spend the money having a good time. We heard she went to Vegas, spent it all, and returned two weeks later to pick up her toddler. We made sure those kids had presents at Christmas, and we sat with them and read stories.

I took my guitar into the hospital to play and sing for my special patient and friend, Wanda Big Crow and her little girls. Despite a resolving case of laryngitis, I managed to do okay and share some holiday spirit. Wanda surprised me with a gift of pillowcases. That was a huge present from someone who had so little, and it meant a lot to me. On my way out, I played a few more songs for others who had heard me from down the hall and wanted more music.

In a season of strong holiday traditions, and coming from a food-centric family, I'm surprised that I can't recall a Christmas dinner that year. I know we made some cookies from family recipes that smelled up the house in December. But maybe because I didn't have access to our traditional Swedish foods, whatever we ate wasn't memorable to me on that particular day. Or maybe we didn't have a special dinner due to crazy work schedules. But even without holiday dinner memories, that Christmas in Rosebud was one of my most meaningful and touching. We had given of ourselves to others, and we felt the true spirit of the season.

Canteyuke

8. Comings and goings

WISDOM. *WOKSAPE (WO-KSA-PEH).* TO UNDERSTAND WHAT IS RIGHT AND TRUE, TO USE KNOWLEDGE WISELY.

Keeping good staff at Rosebud has always been a challenge, due to its remote location and the unique complexity of needs. Even during my brief thirteen months there I witnessed lots of turnover.

Like the nurses, several of our small assembly of doctors were also newly minted. Some of these doctors had joined the Public Health Service as alternative service to the military draft and the Vietnam War. We saw these young men as competent, compassionate, creative, and at least as overworked as we nurses were. But although most had arrived several months before we had, many also had little experience and we now know that they were perpetually scared and insecure too. They read medical books all the time, often just before having to face doing a new procedure. Dr. Tosi recalls attending his first Cesarean birth, with spinal anesthesia. He had never done a cesarean nor administered a spinal, nor had the other available doc, so they flipped a coin, read madly, and did what had to be done. Mother and baby were fine. Another time a patient named Moses Snow Horse came in with a GI bleed and needed surgery to control it. Unbeknown to us nurses, the docs drew straws to see who would administer the anesthesia, since they had never been trained to do this. Dr. Tosi took out the bleeding part of the patient's stomach, and both patient and doctor survived. I think the Great Spirit watched over all of us, knowing we were doing the best we could and that our intentions were honorable.

Dr. Tosi said that one day some Indians told him that they wanted to see the docs grow beards, since most Native Americans have only sparse facial hair and were unable to grow their own. The docs obliged, and gradually took on a look like the Smith Brothers of the cough drop fame (or the men of *Duck Dynasty,* as a more recent example).

Rosebud remains plagued by much depression, one of the highest rates of suicide and homicide in the country, and rampant alcoholism among a myriad of other psychosocial problems. The suicide rate is two to three times the national average per National Relief Charities and St. Francis Mission Suicide Prevention, depending on age breakdown. Many believe that these mental health problems are a direct result of generations of gross mistreatment under federal policy. We were lucky at Rosebud to get one of the three psychiatrists in the state of South Dakota. Dr. Romero's gentle spirit and expertise were sorely needed in this land of desperation.

The psych department consisted of a trailer outside of the hospital. Unfortunately, since there was never enough medical staff, poor Dr. Romero was amazed and chagrinned to soon learn that he had to take general on-call medical duties as well. Judy was on duty the night he had to deliver a baby. He said he hadn't done this since medical school, about a dozen years before. Judy recalled standing behind him while he seemed at a complete loss. Judy told him, "Now just put your hands down there have her push and we'll catch this baby." He just wanted to be the psychiatrist he was trained to be. He stayed only a few months, presumably just until he could find a better spot to land. He told the other docs that he had concluded that Rosebud suffered from a personality disorder. Shortly after Dr. Romero's departure, our remaining mental health worker Clement Whirlwind Soldier took his own life. Sadly, I was just getting to know him.

Rosebud hired a grouchy obstetrician in his forties. He got mad when folks came in at 2 a.m. with sore throats, after travelling all day from remote areas to try to get to the hospital. It seemed he preferred to deliver babies, and shared Dr. Romeros' aversion to practicing outside of his own specialty. He was rude and would yell at patients. Someone shot at his house and he left.

Late in the fall we got our first nursing supervisor, hired for the evening shift. What a concept to actually have someone overseeing the chaos of the busy entire hospital. Mrs. Pilley was a petite middle-aged dynamo, with a take-charge bluster, but also a mentoring attitude to help the new nurses grow, and a glimmer of humor to see us all through. Dr. Tosi recalls that no matter what was going on with a patient, any comment he made was met by her reply, "That's what the sailor said to the French girl," making it sound risqué.

One chilly evening shortly after her arrival, she was detained down in the busy ER for most of the shift. They sent us an admission, a woman named Jackie who was five months pregnant. She had been drinking and was admitted for observation due to some erratic behavior. She was placed not on the maternity side, but instead she went into our observation and isolation room. Located at the far end of the long hall, it had a window in the locked door, plus an entrance foyer and exhaust fan for TB isolation. Jackie settled in pretty quietly, and we initially took turns checking on her or at least looking in the window every 15 to 30 minutes. She appeared to be asleep. Then the floor got very busy with several emergencies, and it was over an hour before we got a chance to check on her again. The aide returned to the desk, looking worried, to report that the patient was not in the room or in the adjoining bathroom, but that the bed sheets had been tied together, hooked to the bed frame, and leading out the open tiny second story window into the cold night. We had taken Jackie's clothes, so she was only wearing a short hospital gown, and had a five-month pregnant belly to squeeze through the small 2 ft. square window. When we got over our shock and amazement regarding the escape, we had to face the potential wrath of our new supervisor. I called to report the situation, and she asked if there was a body at the bottom of the sheets? No? "Then it will have to wait! We're really busy down here in the ER!" Several months later, after the birth of her baby, Jackie was hired as a nurses' aide on the same unit, and we found ourselves curiously dependent on her as part of our care giving team for a while.

In late October one of our best nurses, tall, dark-haired Lynn Romanowski left us to get married in California. She had worked in Rosebud for over a year, and was always a great comfort to have around, both as a nurse at work, but also as a friend. Though I hadn't known her long, and she was only a few years older than me, she seemed like a font of wisdom. I always felt better after talking with her on any topic or when working with her. One day, a guy came out of the psychiatric observation room holding a knife and walking toward the nurses' station. Judy was recalling from class that the proper way to handle the situation was to appear as large as possible and to speak loudly and firmly, and that the patient would likely obey. As Judy was thinking about this, Lynn suddenly stepped out from the desk with her hands on her hips, expanding her tall frame, and said loudly, "Put that knife down and get back in your room!" And he did. Lynn had a gorgeous fluffy white Samoyed dog with bright blue eyes, sweet Dosti, and we would all miss him too. We held several farewell parties, and then Lynn was gone, leaving a sadly empty space.

Dr. Tosi recalls that Joe Eagle Elk was our janitor, and he was also a medicine man. One day a psychiatric patient jumped on his back, and Joe quietly kept mopping the floor. Joe was managing to stay centered and calm as ever.

Good coworkers and a sense of humor are the keys to surviving in a tough job environment. Julie Emory, a local LPN from the Rosebud tribe, graced us with her soft brown eyes, brown hair, a musical laugh and positive energy. She was a wonderful nurse and a joy to have on the unit. She worked there when I came and remained when I left. Her predictable presence was always a stabilizing influence, which deserves mention as any quality stable staff was unusual.

Rosemarie (Rose) Rouch has been mentioned previously, but it was a good thing she came from Indiana when she did, the first week of December. With dark gently waving hair and full rosy cheeks, she resembled Snow White. She was a quiet, but warm and cheery young nurse with a wonderful laugh. We hit it off immediately and she became my cribbage-playing buddy. We played many games together, and she taught me the game of Euchre as well. She comforted me greatly as friction and tension with Judy escalated in her preparations to leave.

Judy was leaving not just to be with her fiancé Russ, but also because she was so frustrated with the administration and conditions at the hospital. She had come to believe that she would be more effective in making changes from outside Rosebud than from working inside the hospital. She had written to the PHS regional office in Aberdeen about some of her concerns. For instance, the uterine infection rate after delivering babies was very high. When brought to our hospital nursing director's attention, Montilou said that the new mothers probably were not washing carefully at home. But Judy pointed out that we nurses were always going into the delivery room for supplies that were not stocked on the floor, and therefore the delivery room was contaminated. Montilou did not see this as a problem, until we cultured the delivery table, sheets, and floor, and everything grew staphylococcus bacteria. Montilou told us to be more careful, but still did not make supplies available out on the floor in a more convenient place. It was also probably relevant that the delivery table was rusty, so no matter how well we scrubbed it, some germs were likely to stay. This kind of thing drove Judy nuts.

Judy tells about caring for Steven F., a twenty-seven-year-old vibrant young man, with a classic face, long black hair, and an athletic body. He was friends with one of Lorna's sons and may have been a dancer too. He came to the ER not feeling well. He was admitted at ten p.m. with nausea, dizziness, and high blood sugar. Alert and talking at first, he'd wanted someone with him. He was a diabetic, and Judy was called in from home to monitor and stay with him. An IV was started, but very little lab work was done due to lack of equipment.

Judy says, "We knew his blood sugar was over 250, but things went from bad to worse and he went into a coma. He just faded away. They couldn't get his blood sugar under control and despite the best care we could give; he was dead by two a.m. Would this have happened anywhere else?"

Rosemary H. was another of the memorable nurses who worked with us. She came from a Blackfoot tribe in Montana, with a classic dark beauty in addition to being an excellent nurse. Everyone liked working with her, although she kept much to herself. One day she didn't show up for work. Nobody could reach her by phone, so eventually someone went to her house to check on her. Tragically she was found dead, having overdosed on pills. When working with her, none of us ever had a clue that she had been in such pain.

When Rose Rouch had come to us in December, she moved into the middle of a three-unit apartment building next to the hospital. She heard a baby crying in the vacant unit next door. She reported this, and upon inspection nothing was found. This had been Rosemary H.'s apartment, now vacant after her recent death there. A priest was called to bless the building, but the crying continued, stopping only after Rosemary H. was buried and laid to rest. I wonder what would have happened if a medicine man had been called.

Mona Lisa is another patient forever in the hearts of Judy and Stephanie. As Stephanie tells it,

"It was a wild and crazy evening shift on pediatrics, like always, it seemed. Too many IVs, too many sick kids. Judy was working overtime doing special duty with a beautiful little girl in a croup tent."

Before taking her supper-break Judy reported to Steph that the little girl, Mona Lisa was stable. Steph was taking care of all the other sick kids with all their meds and IVs, when a family member asked her to check on Mona Lisa. Her color and breathing were good, and she seemed ok to Steph, so she went on to the next child who needed her. Soon the family called her again. Mona Lisa had then stopped breathing. Steph called a code immediately and Judy and Dr. D. came right away.

But Judy recalls that there were no breathing tubes the right size for Mona Lisa, so they had trouble establishing an airway, and the little girl could not be saved. Everybody was distraught and devastated. Judy felt angry because of the lack of equipment and the possibly needless death of a child. After the failed efforts to save Mona Lisa, the little girl and the bedside were a bloody mess. Montilou was going to let the family go right in. Though broken- hearted, Judy argued and insisted on taking out all the tubes and cleaning up the little girl's body first, so that at least the family would have a more dignified final memory of their young daughter. Tall, quiet Dr. D. was also grief-stricken and disappeared for a little while to compose himself.

Judy's letter to the regional office had not been ignored. The day that the contingent from the Aberdeen office came to follow up on her letter was a wild day. Judy was crazy busy on pediatrics, actually doing CPR on two five-month-old babies at once. She had one hand on each baby's chest doing compressions on one baby girl and one baby boy. As Judy tells it:

"The baby girl was already in the hospital that October day when she ran into problems. And then the little baby boy came up from the ER having difficulty breathing. The little boy was the fifth child of a couple whose other four children had all died before the age of eighteen months. Up to this point, the parents had frustrated the doctors by not allowing any autopsies. So, on this day, while the parents stoically sat in the hallway with relatives and watched through a window while we performed CPR, they were asked and finally agreed to airlift these children to Fort Collins, Colorado, for further evaluation. The baby boy died. I have no recollection of how the decision was made, but it was instantaneously decided to keep the CPR going until the transport team came to get this baby to Ft. Collins. We hoped the parents would agree to an autopsy off the reservation. And that's exactly what happened. The child was found to have a congenital heart defect. I didn't stay at Rosebud long enough to know if the parents had a sixth child, but I always hoped that if they did, this child would be sent off the reservation to be evaluated immediately so that a sixth death could be avoided. It was a horrible day, but the little girl survived, and hopefully there was promise for the boy's parents to have the chance to be a family."

Judy never got a chance to talk to the folks from Aberdeen on that impossibly hectic day. But she did write to a prominent columnist at the Washington *Post*, who later wrote an article about Rosebud in the national press.

Stephanie was also a huge support to both Judy and me during this time in early winter. One night I had been to her house for dinner and an evening of embroidering together. Walking home, as I was jolted from her cozy rooms by the crisp cold night, I noticed a halo glowing around a nearby hill. It followed the hill's silhouette as I walked, but teasingly hid the actual moon from view. I passed our own house, drawn in by the light, with my arms fill of sewing items. I crossed the road and climbed a small knoll of high grass, to be rewarded with a glimpse of a huge half-moon peeking from behind the hill. Some delicate clouds were swirled to frame one very bright star, as the center of a flower, with others sprinkled and glittering off to the sides. The beauty of nature's soft lighting and faint shadows completely overcame me. For a moment in time I was at peace.

December also brought a pair of older experienced nurses from New Hampshire, both named Mary. We were hopeful that the staffing would improve and we might not have to work so many long hours or extra shifts. The Marys had told us that they had both wanted for many years to come work with the Indians. However, when they began their first day of work we were all surprised. As the night nurse reported to the arriving day staff about the status of each patient, the new Marys reacted to the local Sioux names.

"Hollow Horn Bear in room 13 had her dressing changed and looks good. Eagle Elk in 14 is breathing easier. Shot with Two Arrows in room 15 had a comfortable night."

"Oh my gosh, they still use arrows?" exclaimed one Mary.

A couple of days later, one of the Marys was giving the report:

"Never Misses a Shot in room 22 got his Demerol every 4 hours."

The oncoming nurse remarked, "She seemed better to me yesterday. Was she in a lot of pain?"

"No," Mary replied, "I just thought she never missed a shot so I gave pain shots whenever she was due!"

Apparently, this confusion, along with the challenging conditions at Rosebud were more than they could handle and both Marys left after only five days. So much for their longstanding dream of working with Indians. With them went our most recent hopes of relief from our overworked schedules.

In mid-December, I wrote in my journal, "Tonight I am empty. I despair of ever feeling anything again. To take this seriously, as a permanent feeling, would be absurd I know, but for tonight I do not know from where my inspiration may come." Days later I got phone calls from family and dear friends at home and called it "a soul transfusion." The hard work, desperate situations, and frequent loss of significant people during the brutal cold winter were taking a toll on me.

After Christmas, we held a small bridal shower for Judy at Stephanie's place. We gave her a locally handmade Morning Star quilt that was very colorful and beautiful. The Lakota women are famous for their fine quality of workmanship in these quilts, which have been on exhibit at the Smithsonian Museum in Washington, D.C. We also gave Judy a see-through black negligee as a joke. We all were so tired from work, and so sad that she was leaving, that the party was a bit of a forced festivity. Judy was enthralled with the West, especially the cowboys and Indians. She was the driving force that had brought the two of us to Rosebud, and I had come along riding her coat tails. Her energy, enthusiasm and humor would be dearly missed.

We had learned so much in our first five months at Rosebud, launching our nursing careers to a remarkable start. One night, Judy was working in the emergency room with Dr. Tosi. A woman arrived with dozens of small cuts from shattered glass in an auto accident. She was so drunk she required no other anesthetic. After they cleaned her up, Dr. Tosi told Judy to grab a needle and start suturing. She told him she'd never done this and didn't know how.

He said, "You know how to sew, don't you? It's the same thing – get started!"

And she did.

Like all of us, Judy had had some very challenging patient experiences. But Judy was the idealist who had such conflict with Montilou—"*Where's … your … cap?*"—Prime, our director of nurses. Montilou would hound us about wearing our nurses' caps, even when we'd had the most hellacious shifts and worked overtime. We would go to see her to describe surviving sisteen hours of hell, and she would respond merely, "Where's your cap?" Judy had the idea to culture our caps for germs, and although we did wash and starch them periodically, they grew large amounts of bacteria. With the cultured cap results, Montilou stopped ordering us to wear the stupid caps that kept getting in our way, knocking into the patient privacy screens around the beds as we tried to give care. Though we had recently been so proud to receive these caps, and later our graduate stripes of ribbon symbolizing our completed nursing education, in the real world of nursing we were glad to leave them home allowing us to work less encumbered. But these battles cost Judy much energy and angst. Regretfully she had finally had enough, so her fiancé Russell came and took her in the little brown Maverick to his family farm in New York.

As Rosebud would have it, Judy actually left a day late, on January fourth rather than the third. She got a stomach bug that kept her from travelling when she had planned. Besides, it was so cold that the car wouldn't start. By evening she was feeling better, so she and Russ visited in Susan Beeson's trailer which had by then been moved from Mission to Rosebud. Judy recalls scratching her name on the frost inside the windows of the trailer there just before leaving.

We sang one last chorus of her favorite Rosebud cowboy song together and she was gone.

"When it's roundup time in Rosebud and the bloom is on the sage

How I long to be in Rosebud, back a-riding on the range

Just to hear those coyotes whining, calling to me from above

To be free again, just to be again in dear old Rosebud."

Woksape.

9. Wanda

HUMILITY. *UNSIICIYAPI (UN-SHEE-EE-CEE-YAH-PEE)*. TO BE HUMBLE, MODEST, UNPRETENTIOUS.

Wanda Big Crow would come to the Rosebud hospital after her husband had beaten her severely, once running over her with the car. I never met her husband, but she said he was nasty when drunk. Wanda was about my age, and she boomeranged in and out of the hospital several times in my year at Rosebud. Sometimes she stayed for weeks or months.

Since Wanda spent so much time with us, we came to know her pretty well. She had two little girls, about four and seven years old. Her mother, Alice Four Horns cared for them whenever Wanda was unable to do so. I was just beginning my nursing career, and I had a limited understanding of the cycle of domestic violence, and a steep learning curve about alcoholism.

Because many Native Americans, like Asians, lack an enzyme to metabolize alcohol efficiently, their bodies may react differently, increasing its effects. On any given day, about 90 percent of our ER patients had alcohol-related complaints: liver disease, pancreatitis, DTs, fetal alcohol syndrome, domestic violence, neglect, auto accidents, gastritis, diabetes, and alcoholic dementia, for example. The social complexities of poverty, depression, generations of trauma, and challenges of life on the reservation in addition to this missing enzyme compounded the risk of alcoholism, which was rampant. There were very few resources in Rosebud and little hope of any effective treatment back in 1973. Today, Rosebud still remains a part of the second poorest county in the U.S.

Wanda would come in with severe bruises and broken bones, but it was pancreatitis and internal injuries that were the cause of her extended stays with us. She displayed a strength of spirit, a flashing sweet smile, and a goodness that drew us in. As Christmas approached, she confided from her hospital bed her concern that she couldn't shop for her girls. She was too sick, plus there was no money, and of course in 1973 online shopping had yet to be invented. A nurse needs to build a professional wall in order to remain objective in caring for patients. But occasionally a patient sneaks through the cracks in the wall and touches your heart. Judy and I decided to help.

We bought the few modest things Wanda wanted to get for her girls, plus some of our own gift ideas.

Wanda went home after a few weeks, but she returned later in the winter. Her condition then deteriorated so much that she was transported to the medical center in Lincoln, Nebraska. I don't think she had ever been away from Rosebud before, so being off the rez with strangers compounded her stress.

I decided to visit her with my friend Stephanie. Not surprisingly, the Rosebud hospital remained short-staffed, so we were only given 24 hours to make the trip. It should take eight hours each way, plus visit time. We planned to drive and sleep in shifts. But Mother Nature had other plans for us.

We left at 11 p.m., after work, in Stephanie's little cherry-red Chevy Vega subcompact. About midnight it started snowing and blowing. We drove on. The radio always aired frequent winter reminders to carry a blanket and emergency chocolate bar, in case of being stranded in sudden winter storms. Packing the blanket was no problem, but the chocolate somehow kept disappearing. The snow came down heavier, and the wind strengthened across the high plains—a real surprise blizzard. We could barely see past the large flying flakes in the headlights. The wipers began freezing up and the snow was starting to drift as the wind rocked us. By now we had driven far from anywhere, so on we ventured with the defroster and heat cranked up in the subzero night on the open prairie until we could go no further. The wheels had gotten stuck in a high drift and we couldn't get out. The radio had said nothing about carrying a shovel. We tried rocking and pushing the car, but it was too deep and slick. We were definitely stuck. At about two in the morning, no other traffic braved the stormy interstate. The snow kept piling up fast, to the door handles now, and starting to cover the windows as we huddled inside the little red car.

At age twenty-two, we acutely felt our mortality for the first time. We found ourselves faced with the choice of turning off the engine and freezing to death or staying warm but suffocating to death from carbon monoxide poisoning. We decided to split the difference and alternate intervals of each. Our fingers, toes, and noses were tingling with cold as the wind howled in the frigid night. We turned on the heat with windows cracked for a while to defrost ourselves, then closed the windows with the engine off. We dozed, and then awakened to a scraping noise. Around six in the morning the truckers had started coming through, and one alert, kind soul had seen the top of the little red car and dug us out. With great relief and thankful hearts, we drove the hour to Sioux Falls, the nearest town. Checking into a motel shortly past dawn, we two young women were eyed suspiciously and were told to sleep in separate beds. We found this an ironic contrast to when Steph and Judy had gotten stranded in Pierre and were told to share a bed so they wouldn't dirty the extra sheets. Even though it was still early morning, we figured we had earned a drink to celebrate our survival. Since we were in the Big City, compared to Rosebud, we'd try something exotic like a grasshopper, made with crème de menthe, crème de cocoa, and I think vodka. We thought we were so sophisticated. We found a bar that was open, but when we ordered, they asked,

"What's a grasshopper?"

All they could offer was 3.2 beer in that big city. That was breakfast. A quick nap in our separate beds and then we needed to return for our next shift at Rosebud. We never did get to visit Wanda Big Crow in Lincoln, but at least we lived to tell the tale.

Alice Four Horns was so grateful for the care and support during her daughter's illnesses that she invited me to a Yuipi ceremony to help heal Wanda. This is a very special prayer ritual where a medicine man is tied up in a quilt and spirits are manifested as little lights in the darkness. I was very honored and excited to be included and dearly wanted to go, but again Mother Nature had other ideas. I got my period that day and therefore would interfere with the power of the healing spirits. I briefly considered not telling anyone and going anyway, but I didn't want to jeopardize the ceremony or be disrespectful. I never did get to go to a Yuipi ceremony, and even today I still would love to go. As a thank you for my care, Wanda's brother made me a fine yellow beaded medallion necklace, and Alice made me some orange beaded spiral earrings, with the tiniest of beads.

When I later left Rosebud, Wanda promised she would stay in touch with me. I wrote to her several times, but never heard back. I was disappointed, but not entirely surprised. Writing letters to outsiders was really not part of the Rosebud culture. I've thought of Wanda over the years, wondering, and wishing her well.

Unsiiciyapi.

16. Wanda, Alice and the girls.

10. Carriacou getaway

LOVE. *CANTOGNAKE (CHAN-DOE-GNAN-KEH)*. TO PLACE AND HOLD IN ONE'S HEART.

"Don't come STOP Revolution in progress STOP Travel too dangerous STOP"

This was the one and only telegram I ever received in my life. The man I wanted to marry had gone into the Peace Corps on the tiny Caribbean island of Carriacou and I had gone to great lengths planning my visit from Rosebud. My reply telegram said, "Crazy Swede on the way STOP I'll see how far I can get STOP"

Tom (or Tommmm as my mother called him) had played lead guitar and I had sung at the folk mass at the University of Connecticut. Sometimes we'd performed for weddings and coffeehouses together. He stood at 5'10" with thick brown hair, blue eyes, and spoke with a gentle voice that could melt my heart. When we graduated from college in the spring of 1973, he left for the Peace Corps without making promises, knowing that communication would be challenging over the next couple of years. He was teaching on an island only seven square miles in size, mostly without electricity or running water. The mail boat circled through only once or twice a week. Tom liked to say that if everyone hung their laundry out at the same time the island would sail away.

By the following February I missed him terribly, especially in the lonely cold winter of Rosebud, and had decided to visit. We had managed to exchange a few letters and to keep the flame alive. So, I called the nearest AAA office 220 miles away in Sioux Falls, for a travel agent to help me figure out logistics. I'd never traveled anywhere by myself. It took two weeks before the agent called back to report triumphantly that he had found both Rosebud and Carriacou on the map! Now he could start planning the flights, and I eagerly waited to hear how I would make my journey. Plane changes would occur in Chicago, Atlanta, San Juan, and St Lucia. Miraculously, I got the travel time approved at work, even though the hospital was still as short staffed as ever.

But when the actual travel week finally arrived, so did Tom's telegram. The revolution concerned Grenada's independence from the British Commonwealth, along with nearby Carriacou, an island of Grenada. People were rioting, and broken glass littered the runway.

By then, I had made up my mind, being a stubborn Swede, and a Taurus to boot. My time had been approved and I needed to get away from work for a while. I decided to try to reach Carriacou. If I could only make it part way, I was prepared with my beading loom and supplies, books, and things to keep me busy on some sunny beach. But I really missed Tom, and I wanted to see where he was living and to meet his friends.

Bright and early, a friend drove me the hundred miles to the nearest commercial airport in Pierre, to catch the first flight to Chicago. Dressed in a baby blue clingy pantsuit, I had lost a little weight for the reunion and was feeling pretty good about my appearance. I hadn't left Rosebud since arriving the previous August. I boarded the plane and the businessman seated beside me politely asked what I did. When I started telling him about where I worked, it opened a floodgate of information about life in Rosebud. I don't think he was able to squeeze in another word for the entire flight. I hadn't realized how much frustration, anger, horror, and yet respect and fascination I had pent up inside me. The poor guy probably would never ask that question again.

I waited several hours in Chicago enjoying a good lunch and exploring O'Hare airport. I checked on flights to Carriacou and so far, so good. I called my mom from Atlanta around bedtime in Connecticut to report that we were again in the same time zone. She knew where I was heading, but I hadn't told her about the revolution. She didn't ask so I guess the news hadn't reached her. My late flight to San Juan arrived around two in the morning. I tried to check on flights to Carriacou, but things wouldn't open until six, so I tried to nap. Promptly at six I was the first in line at Travelers' Aid where they reported that the flights were still ok. But by the time I got that information, my plane had left for St. Lucia with my luggage. I desperately scrambled to find another flight. The next one wasn't until suppertime, but it was my only option, so I booked that one. I debated whether to go out and see some of San Juan, but I didn't want to get lost. So, I hung out at the airport all day, listening to the mariachi band, trying new foods in the cafeteria, and talking with a few fellow travelers. One guy from Port-au-Prince tried to convince me to go with him to Haiti, but I still wanted to get to Carriacou and Tommmmm if I could.

Finally, I caught the evening flight to St. Lucia, unaware of the island's two airports, and sure enough my luggage was at the other one. Arriving about ten p.m., I didn't know anyone and had no place to stay. The small airport offered very few services. So, with no destination and everything closed at the airport, I got in a shuttle taxi with a group of other travelers. As we drove off I asked where they all were staying. One guy said he was going to a pretty big resort and they might have a room, so that became my plan. The taxi driver then told me that he had a friend who owned a guest house with a vacancy for the night, so I went with him after he dropped off everyone else. This raises many alarms as I write this, but it was a different time, a different world. Plus, I was naïve and trusting. And desperate.

He did bring me to a nice clean friendly little place. The kind woman in charge said I could stay that night but that I would have to leave the next day as they would then be full. Without luggage I slept well in my bare essentials. I awakened to the sound of teeming rain, but I opened my eyes to bright dappled sunlight. In confusion, I peered out the window to find that the sound was created by the palm fronds waving against each other in the soft tropical breeze. I was startled by a knock on my door, and the mistress said that I had a visitor. How could this be? I didn't know where I was, and I didn't know anyone there. It was the taxi driver, Charlie, wanting to know if I needed a ride to the airport to go get my luggage and to make travel arrangements!! I felt flabbergasted to see him, but very grateful, as I still had no plan.

Charlie waited comfortably with the innkeepers while I ate breakfast. Then we set out for the airport. We found my previously unclaimed suitcase, but learned that the situation on Carriacou had deteriorated, and now my flight had been canceled. What to do? Mail boat? It had just left and wouldn't go again for a few days, using up my vacation. Hmm. Somehow, I got the idea to charter a plane. I checked with LIAT, the airline that had cancelled my flight, and while they wouldn't fly commercially, they would do a private charter. But their smallest available plane held nine passengers. Surprisingly I could afford this charter, since I was working my first real job without much to spend money on at Rosebud. I'd made it this far, so why not keep going? I booked a charter for the next morning, the soonest they would go.

Meanwhile, I thought that since we had nine plane seats to fill I'd try to make some of my money back. I made an announcement at the airport that anyone interested in sharing a charter to Carriacou should come see me standing in a particular corner. After a few minutes, a six-foot blond surfer airhead dude ambled over. He said he'd always wanted to go to Carriacou and he'd heard the snorkeling was fantastic there. So, he was in. But he had no money to pay for it. Well, I was going anyway. By the way, did he know a place I could stay that night? He replied that he and his buddy would be out partying, so I could stay at their place and they wouldn't bother me. Ok—desperate times—I would take him up on the offer. Nobody else seemed interested in sharing the charter so we headed back to the taxi. Surfer Dude directed Charlie to drive us to where he was staying. To my great amazement we found ourselves back at the same guest house I'd just left! And then for the second time the matron told me that I had a visitor. Again, I hadn't known where I had been going, and I sure didn't know anyone else on the island. This time I was surprised by a young pilot who had heard my announcement at the airport. He said he could fly us in his two-passenger plane for half the price that LIAT was charging for the nine-seater. Ok. Good deal. I'll take it. He promised to pick us up in the morning.

Now that we had retrieved my suitcase and bathing suit, Charlie generously offered to take me to the beach for the afternoon. In return I treated him to dinner. I settled in for the night, alone, as promised. In the morning, the pilot came to get me along with Surfer Dude. The pilot brought a young friend who he said was, "learning to navigate."

At the airport the guys went to get the plane. Then to my dismay I saw through the window that they were pulling a tiny toy-size plane by a clip-on wagon-like handle. This appeared to be the ride I had bartered and chartered. Surfer Dude and I crawled on board behind the pilot and his aspiring navigator. As the little yellow propeller spun and we were poised to take off, the control tower stopped us. It turned out that it was illegal to charter a single engine plane over water, in case the one and only engine conks out. LIAT had found out about my new charter deal and had reported us. In my excitement I hadn't cancelled my nine-seater charter with LIAT, but then they hadn't notified me when they had cancelled my earlier flight either, so I felt we were even. Anyway, the new pilot managed to convince the control tower that we were simply old friends and that it was not really a charter, so off we flew. It seemed we were required to stop for customs at every little leeward island between St. Lucia and Carriacou. Surfer Dude was feeling the effects of his partying and needed the barf bag with all the ups and downs. At one point our aspiring navigator could identify neither the island below, nor the radio frequency to find out. I heard him say, "I can't tell if it's Palm Island or Carriacou." We watched the goats clear from the dirt runway and we landed. The pilot stuck his head out the tiny window, asking, "Is this Carriacou?"

The airport official replied "Yes," and we had arrived.

We hopped out of our trusty little plane and walked to the tiny cinder block shack that served as Carriacou's airport to go through customs. I had yet to pay the pilot for our illegal charter, and I was worried that I might need this guy for a ride back due to the revolution. We had very little time left as the pilot was getting back into the plane to return. I quickly told the customs agent that I needed to say goodbye to "my friend." I ran back out to the airstrip and shook the pilot's hand through the tiny window, smoothly passing him the wadded cash from my hand and getting his contact info in case I needed a return ride.

The next task was finding Tom, as I had been writing only to a post office box. I asked someone where the white Peace Corps guys lived and easily got a ride to the house. I knocked, with Surfer Dude standing behind me, and Tom answered the door, with his Peace Corps friend Aileen standing behind him. Awkward. He said he hadn't received my telegram saying that I was coming. I was thinking that it was a very good thing I'd made the trip. In the months of tropical sun, Tom's brown hair had bleached to copper and he was covered in bronzy freckles from hours of snorkeling and spear fishing. Aileen excused herself and went home, but it took us several days to lose the freeloading Surfer Dude.

I reconnected with Tom, watching him teach, going on beach walks, hosting guitar parties and learning to snorkel. He caught lobster and fish for me, served with limes from the tree just outside. He and his roommates had a goat and a puppy named Frodo, who would chase each other all through the yard and into the house, playing king of the hill on the couch. Unfortunately, Frodo rooted through my suitcase while we were at school and chewed my diaphragm. This caused some initial panic, but even so, we managed to have a lovely visit. Interestingly, we found common threads in our work settings, with the culture of poverty and the widespread use of drums in both Rosebud and Carriacou.

The next year I returned by a more direct route starting from Cheyenne, Wyoming, but I deliberately arranged to travel again via St Lucia. I was met at the airport by Charlie my taxi driver friend, and another man came running up saying, "Remember me? I'm St. George. I carried your suitcase!" We all went out to dinner and to the beach before I continued on to Carriacou. I'm pleased to report that Tommmmm and I were married in 1978 and we have since lived happily ever after.

Cantognake.

17. Pilot and Surfer Dude with charter plane and wagon handle.

11. Beach day

FORTITUDE. *CANTEWASAKE (CAN-TE-WAH-SHA-KEH)*. STRENGTH OF HEART AND MIND.

As spring brought the return of the warmer weather, Stephanie and I both longed for the beach. We had both grown up on the East Coast, Steph near Baltimore and I near Hartford. We were feeling landlocked and claustrophobic in the middle of the vast Great Plains. A real beach day getaway seemed very unlikely, so we used our Rosebud creativity and thought of the Nebraska sand hills, which were a couple of hours away by car. If we couldn't have the sea, at least we could have the sand. We sure needed a little break from the stressful rigors of our daily routine.

During the long winter, temperatures often dropped to 40 below with the chill wind howling across the prairie. Snow drifts could easily reach ten feet. People burned tires in the living rooms of their government *Sioux 400* shacks to try to stay warm, if they had housing at all. Others lived in cars and broke the ice in the creeks to wash themselves. Gangrene feet and extremities were not unusual sights at the hospital. Bodies were even brought into the emergency room that were frozen in a seated position, having died waiting in their broken-down cars for help. A public health nurse had shown me a whole town without a water source. Local ranchers might comment about "those dirty Indians," but the ranchers weren't the ones trying to wash in a frozen creek, like in the old traditional ways. I'd heard that many people living in the shacks had even pulled out the copper pipes to sell for cash, as many of the pipes had never been hooked up anyway. The extreme poverty in Rosebud differed from poverty back East. Here it was so remote and destitute that resources were scarce or nonexistent. No Salvation Army or Goodwill, no thrift stores or hand-me-downs. Without enough to go around in the first place, there was little to pass on.

Even with such limited basic human necessities, the Sioux culture has kept a tradition called the Giveaway. Generosity is one of the key values of the Lakota culture. People would organize a big party to celebrate friendship, an anniversary, or other important event, and give out valuable new gifts to their guests. I was impressed by the generosity of these people who were struggling mightily to scrape by for their daily needs.

Transportation offered yet another challenge in the vast prairie, as the majority of people did not have cars or trucks, and no bus or public transport of any kind. Most families had no phones or any modern way of contacting others for a ride anyway.

One early Sunday morning as I was walking up the hill to church I saw an old man limping ahead of me. I caught up with him and he told me he'd just been discharged from the hospital after being treated for a beating the previous night. He was walking home to Parmalee, which was 15 miles away. I joined him, and as he requested, we stopped at the police station to get him some salted nuts for nourishment. Who knew the police station had such things to share? We walked the remaining short distance to church together. Afterward, he waited while I walked home to make him a sandwich and then brought my car to take him to Parmalee. He wanted to stop along the way to visit several people and show them his new friend. Before this, I simply hadn't even thought about how patients got home when we discharged them. I had been only aware of another empty bed soon to be filled.

We had pregnant women who came in to the hospital a couple of weeks before delivery and stayed, just waiting, because they'd walked the ten or fifteen miles from their towns of He Dog or Upper Cut Meat. They wanted to be sure their baby would be born at the hospital. Stephanie and Dr. Tosi commented on cultural variations in expressing labor pain. Both of them were trained in vocal Hispanic communities, where they could tell the labor was progressing as the laboring mothers' cries got louder. Dr. Tosi says he almost missed his first delivery in Rosebud because the stoic Lakota women rarely cry out, even without drugs. But he learned to notice that delivery is imminent when there is a telltale sheen of sweat on the upper lip. Rose recalls a young eighteen-year-old first-time mother in labor. As her contractions intensified, she started moaning and crying. Her mother was sitting nearby and leaned over to say, "Shut up! Do you want people to think you're a white woman?" The eighteen-year-old gained instant control over her pain and became quiet. She didn't need any Lamaze classes or breathing techniques. It soon became obvious to Rose that this method of pain management was well known among all laboring mothers on the reservation. Bravery and fortitude are greatly valued in the Lakota tradition.

Those few who did own cars or trucks kept them going far beyond normal circumstances. Those vehicles were known as rezmobiles. The roads were very tough in the extremes of weather, and many small communities were accessed by unpaved rutted washboard roads which were punishing to cars. Reservation roads were said to be like government promises: full of holes. When it rained, the mud was known as sticky gumbo. Reservation mechanics and the owners of rezmobiles showed extreme creativity and resourcefulness. For example, Eustice Nightshield had somehow been trained by the government to be a piano tuner, though I can't imagine a big demand for his services because I never saw a piano in Rosebud. He drove a car without any forward gears, so he went everywhere in reverse. But he got there. Dr. Tosi recalls seeing a sign in one area reading "Rubber Tires Only," which made sense only after he saw another car driving on its rims with no tires. But even the trusty rezmobiles did have their limits. One night in the ER, a pedestrian came in after being hit by a *phantom car* with no lights and no motor, just coasting downhill—maybe no brakes either. People could freeze to death in a stranded rezmobile, as it was often easily twenty miles between towns and forty-below in the winter. Dr. T. bought airplane landing lights to mount on the fender of his Bronco, since without any posted speed limit he didn't want to hit anyone or anything when he was going eighty miles an hour on these roads. Even when the rezmobiles finally cannot be mobilized any longer, the rusting hulks are often permanently parked in the yard and can be used as dog houses or other forms of shelter or shade from the unrelenting prairie sun of the blazing hot summers.

I made a daily trek to the post office hoping for mail from friends and family, and especially from Tom. We all spent much time and energy reaching out from Rosebud by writing or calling loved ones, but Tom had only one phone on his entire island, and it was not his to use. He also said that the mail boat came only once or twice a week. Plus, the revolution had caused a blockade for several weeks, with nothing going in or out. A Beach Day might just help me to feel closer to Tom on his tropical island. On a day when there was no mail for me, the postal clerk saw the disappointment in my face and he felt so sorry for me that he gave me a handful of junk mail. The sad part is I was grateful for the gesture, and maybe even for the junk mail itself.

Mothers' Day weekend carried a different meaning in Rosebud. Rather than the lovely annual May holiday honoring mothers, here it referred to the time when the monthly welfare checks were cashed. For many, the cash was quickly converted into alcohol. On those weekends the hospital would be hopping with patients needing treatment for drunken beatings, motor vehicle accidents, liver failure, uncontrolled diabetes, neglected children, and a whole gamut of alcohol-related problems. We could easily get seven admissions on each Mothers' Day weekend eight-hour shift. Dr. Tosi remembers a man walking into the ER with a baseball hat hanging at his waist. The hat was placed to conceal a knife stuck into his abdomen up to the hilt. He had hung the hat because he didn't want to scare anyone. He was obese and luckily the knife only penetrated fat layers, so he recovered well from his wound.

Another patient came in drunk and delirious after a motor vehicle accident. Dr. Tosi recalls that his scalp had been mostly detached by the trauma from glass and metal. Yet he needed no anesthesia with all the alcohol in his system. Dr. Tosi worked to sew the patient back together with Charlie White, the Lakota physician's assistant whom he was mentoring. The patient kept calling the doctor a draft dodger and a coward. Charlie egged him on. The patient pulled the sterile drape off to attack Dr. Tosi, but then Charlie stepped in and stopped him so they were able finish sewing him back together safely.

One incident involved an eighty-year-old bootlegger, Pearl Comes Out Hawk, a white woman married to an Indian. Since the reservation was supposedly dry, she ran grain alcohol the fifty miles in from Valentine, Nebraska to Rosebud. Someone banged on her door one night wanting alcohol, and he kept banging after she told him to go away. So, she shot him in the face with a twenty-two-caliber gun. The ER doc noticed remarkably little blood, and the man told him that his mouth had been open when he'd been shot. The bullet miraculously had ricocheted off a molar and had landed in his cheek, causing only minor damage.

Rose recalls one instance where alcohol actually was beneficial. A woman in her second trimester of pregnancy was having pre-term contractions. The doctor had told his wife to bring a bottle of their whiskey and a shot glass to the hospital. Rose was instructed to have the patient drink two shots of whiskey, followed by another shot every half hour until the labor stopped or she became drunk. Though Rose had not been taught this in her OB nursing classes, she did as the doctor ordered. And it worked. The patient's contractions stopped, and after a good night's rest she went home with her yet-to-be-born baby. In fact, IV alcohol drips were an accepted medical treatment for pre-term labor at the time (but Rosebud had no IV alcohol). Given the amount of alcohol consumed by our population, Rosebud did experience a very low rate of prematurity. However, unfortunately, we did note a high rate of fetal alcohol syndrome, which is still a major issue there today.

Sexual abuse was another rampant problem, even victimizing little children. A particularly nasty man repeatedly beat his wife and raped a five-year-old girl, possibly his niece. Dr. Tosi had to sew up the little girl in the ER. Dr. Tosi testified in court. But the man was repeatedly allowed to go free because the court felt he was not a flight risk since he only had a rezmobile, and no reliable transportation to get very far. The family became angry with Dr. Tosi for testifying. Another time, Dr. Tosi got a call from the local priest asking to borrow his sleeping bags so he could take the local kids camping, "so they wouldn't see the hanging."

Dr. Tosi asked, "What hanging?"

Apparently during the time that American Indian Movement had taken over the tribal police cars they planned to hang a different man who had repeatedly raped a number of small girls. He believes the hanging was carried out quietly and without any opposition.

The rampant beatings, violence and alcoholism were big enough problems to keep us busy at the hospital, in addition to the illnesses related to poor nutrition and living conditions. But as we became more familiar with these people, a slow realization began to dawn that these were symptoms of deeper trauma related to an entire society's long history of pain from generations of being displaced, attacked, and unable to live their culture. We couldn't change history. All we could do was try to ease the present complaints, with respect and compassion, as patients continued to overwhelm us.

Adding to our challenges were some of the other hospital staff. For example, two older colorful nurses usually took turns working on the smaller pediatrics wing. They would have been entertaining if they hadn't been so annoying. Mrs. Wembly was a lumpy heavyset busybody with a cloud of white hair. She actually invited herself to our apartment and then snooped around on a self-guided tour when we first moved to Rosebud, far beyond the boundaries of a friendly visit. I once stumbled upon her exploring the contents of my dresser.

However, she did know her way around the pediatric floor after so many years, and I was grateful for her expertise when I was first assigned to work on that unit. But that gratitude was quickly replaced with annoyance at all her personal prying, bossiness and unwillingness to actually go to a patient's room. Ms. Alzo reigned as the other matron of pediatrics, a petite gray-haired woman with a facial expression alternating between anxiety and blankness. Her mind worked slowly, and she would drive us nuts especially when she gave medications, spelling each name aloud: "aspirin: A-S-P-I-R-I-N aspirin." Everything else was moving so fast and there she was, slowly processing each painful detail of every critical scene. Help. Get me outta here! I need to get to the beach.

Although many patients showed various complications of alcoholism, some were most dramatic and memorable. One middle-aged woman who appeared to be much older, was dying of cirrhosis and end-stage liver failure. Her jaundiced skin and eyes were a bright yellow and her tight swollen belly looked as though she could give birth to a twenty- pound baby. Her family gathered in vigil at her bedside as her condition worsened and she drifted in and out of consciousness. Then the bleeding began, as her disabled liver could no longer regulate the clotting of her blood, and the belly fluid caused a backup of pressure into her upper GI system. As her family watched transfixed in horror, blood began pouring out of her nose and mouth. There appeared to be no way to stop it. Though at this point the patient remained alert and remarkably calm, the family understandably became increasingly distressed and distraught. In compassion and desperation, Dr. Tosi inserted a Foley urinary catheter up her nose and inflated the balloon at the end in her throat to put pressure on at least some of the hemorrhaging blood vessels. This procedure amazingly did seem to at least slow the visible bleeding, but neither he nor I could stand there indefinitely putting traction on the catheter. We had a hospital full of other patients as well. So, he sent someone to the high school to borrow a football helmet, anchoring the catheter tightly to the facemask to keep pressure on the bleeding sites. We both knew that this woman was dying and beyond our help. But Dr. Tosi's compassion for her frightened and horrified family, who was witnessing this last graphic memory of their loved one, inspired this very creative approach to control the visible bleeding. Although he couldn't save the patient, he made a heroic effort to ease at least the family's trauma and pain.

One rare fall day most of the doctors were away attending a workshop. A bad multiple car wreck occurred near our hospital. The only doc in town was Dr. K., our lean, long-haired hippie doc. He had been too sick to go to the workshop with a fever of 103. After the wreck it was all hands on deck in the emergency room. Dr. K. even left his sick bed to come help us. The metallic smell of blood still stays with me to this day. The non-Indians could not be treated at our Indian hospital, and we had to arrange for them to be transported to the nearest hospitals fifty miles away in either Winner, South Dakota or in Valentine, Nebraska. Some of the remaining Indian patients were airlifted out, some treated and released, and some were admitted. Activity buzzed as we cleaned abrasions, sutured gashes, and picked glass out of wounds for most of the day.

Another day and another car wreck brought in a young pregnant couple, about eight months along. The woman had a stillbirth after the accident, and she asked to see their baby. When I went to clean and wrap the baby for her parents, it was clear that the fragile immature skull had been crushed in the accident. Sadly, I went to the parents and tried to talk them out of seeing their damaged baby, but they were insistent. I tried to carefully arrange the shattered eggshell of skull into some semblance of normal, but it kept cracking and shifting in my hands. Like Humpty Dumpty, it could not be put back together again. I brought the little lost soul with a beautiful face on a crushed head to the room with her parents and we cried together. I will never forget the overwhelming emotions of that day.

After all these challenges, we felt it was so essential to take mental health breaks from the intensity of work, so for our spring Beach Day Steph and I packed our bathing suits, even though the sand hills contained no body of water. We brought blankets, sunscreen, hats, a picnic, books, sunglasses, and off we went. The soft sand molded to our forms as we lay on our blankets in the warm sun. It did feel a little like the beach if we kept our eyes closed to the view of only sand. Of course, we still missed that wonderful salty sea smell, and the sounds of the lapping waves and seagulls. But the breeze soon picked up, filling that silence. We sat up briefly, but the sand had begun to blow, so it felt better lying down to avoid the sand stinging our skin. As the wind increased, unobstructed across the Great Plains, the sand started getting in our hair, ears, eyes, noses, and even our teeth. Sadly, we packed up after less than an hour in the warm sun. We ate our picnic in the protection of the car with the windows up. Actually, it was a good thing we left when we did, as Stephanie has the fair freckled skin that burns so easily. Despite the sunscreen, she developed second degree burns from that fairly brief sun exposure. I think a big component of color for each of us was also the windburn. There's no substitute for a genuine relaxing day at the beach, which includes the sound of the waves, smell of the salty air, and dips in the actual ocean.

Cantewasake.

18. Stephanie carrying my dog, Blue.

12. Budget woes and the volunteers

COMPASSION. *WAUNSILAPI (WAH-UN-SHEE-LAH-PEE)*. TO CARE, TO SYMPATHIZE.

As if times weren't tough enough at the Rosebud Hospital, President Nixon and Congress cut the budget for HEW (Department of Health, Education, and Welfare, predecessor to the Department of Health and Human Services, or HHS), and we ran out of money entirely in the spring of 1974. We had no disposable supplies: no paper cups for giving meds, no paper towels for hand washing, no gloves, no surgical dressings or sanitary pads for the new mothers who delivered babies. We had to send the janitor to the general store to buy paper goods on credit. But for specialized medical items we were stuck. We had to re-use the disposable kit to clean the comatose twelve-year-old boy's tracheostomy, for weeks. We lacked drugs, lab reagents, and x-ray film. How can a hospital function under these conditions?

The new budget wouldn't start until the new fiscal year in July when we expected additional funding. It later occurred to me that this budget crisis was not an isolated event, but a recurring one, whenever Congress delays approval or approves inadequate funds. The Indian Health Service has been underfunded since its origin in 1955. The crisis happens mostly every year until the new budget brings more inadequate funding to start each July.

Rose recalled applying Nitropaste, a topical medication for preventing heart pain. The cream usually came packaged with a small bundle of paper rulers, to measure the proper dose (For example, "apply one inch every six hours.") But not in Rosebud. We never got the paper rulers, and applied the cream, just eyeballing the dose. It was only in a later job when Rose was questioned about the paper ruler for her patient that she learned the proper application of the drug.

Rose also told of working nights, when the lights often flickered off and on. One morning before she left, she asked Virgil, the young good-looking maintenance man for help. There was never any maintenance person working at night. He took her to the basement and showed her the big main power box taking up an entire wall. Plugged into this main box was a flimsy extension cord, with only two prongs and no ground. Virgil told Rose to jiggle the cord, and behold, there was light. The hospital's power supply depended on this precarious arrangement.

Times were so bad that NBC came out to film a documentary of the desperation. However, Rosebud was so remote that it only received one TV station, and that was CBS. Thus, a group of hospital staff drove 50 miles to a motel in Winner, South Dakota, to watch the show. I was never able to see the special since I was on duty when it aired, and this was before the more current technology of recording TV shows. Short-staffed as ever and with no hope of new hires in the budget crisis, once the show aired in prime time, the phone began ringing nonstop. The viewer response was overwhelming, but since it was in the evening the calls came directly to our medical floor. People called from all over the country offering to donate miscellaneous supplies:

"My mother has a walker and a bedpan she isn't using. Do you want that?"

I know the callers meant well, but an aide, an LPN and I were trying to care for our twenty-five patients. We told all the callers to send whatever they could.

I wasn't privy to the financial information, but as a result of that TV documentary we did get several interesting volunteers for the summer. A tall thin older doctor arrived to help in the ER. He was nice enough, but it appears that he may have had some dementia. One Saturday, a young man came in with an injured hand. This doc checked the X-ray, treated and wrapped the hand, and sent him on his way. A couple of hours later the doorbell rang (we had to run down from the patient care floor to cover the ER on weekends) and the young man was back, looking sheepish. He had been hiding in the grass watching and waiting respectfully for the older doc to leave. Good thing the doc took a lunch break. Dr. Whoops had looked at the flip side of the X-ray and mistakenly wrapped the wrong hand. The young man did not want to offend or embarrass the doctor, so he had been patiently waiting, hidden outside. I wrapped his injured hand, and he thanked me and left. Humility and respect are central Lakota values, often a striking aspect of people's behavior.

Another doc was sent to us when the older doc left. He did not seem pleased to be at Rosebud and I don't remember ever seeing him smile. He really was a most unpleasant person. He was Asian, and his strong accent and cultural differences were major barriers to his care for these patients. On one very busy day, the ER was hopping with several patients needing urgent attention. In came a woman in labor, ready to start pushing. He actually told her to cross her legs until he could get to her! I looked into the woman's puzzled and distressed eyes, and we quickly got her up to the delivery room. Dr. Grumpy didn't last long.

We got a couple of young volunteers about our age, too. I can't recall what their duties were, but they were certainly a welcome addition to our barely existent social life, for a couple of months. Lenel, a vivacious young woman in her 20s with long brown hair, played the guitar with me. We played several spontaneous back porch sing-alongs with the neighborhood kids on Pill Hill, the hospital housing area. Brad was a handsome quiet California guy with straight brown hair who enjoyed the outdoors. I think it was his idea for us all to go camping out at Chases Women Lake, a few miles from the hospital. A lovely idea on a fine summer night. Four of us planned to sleep under the stars, which were magnificent in the wide-open sky with no moon or light pollution. We each spread our sleeping bag out on the bristly grass, checking for rattlesnakes first, and hoping they wouldn't come seeking our warmth later in the night. It was too dry to build a campfire, with the real danger of a fire spreading.

We must have brought guitars, but I can only remember another kind of music. After we'd settled in and the talk was fading, I said, "Do you hear that? It sounds like drums."

The drums got louder, and then the chanting and singing began. It sounded pretty close, maybe behind a small bunch of trees. With all the recent unrest, this camping trip was looking like a nice idea gone bad. Then we heard footsteps approaching in the swishing grass. We ducked our heads into our sleeping bags trying to look flat and blend in, or as Jack Crabb said in the movie, *Little Big Man*, "Pretend you're invisible."

We each held our breath, really worried that it might be our last. If this person was drunk and not pleased to find us he could become violent. We heard running water, and then fading footsteps in the moonless night. Exhale. The music continued, as we quietly and quickly packed up, no longer appreciating the beauty of the night. We hightailed it out of there for the safety of home.

Shortly after the young summer volunteers arrived, my college friend Pam Marino visited from Connecticut for a week. On the way back from picking her up at the airport in Pierre, she remarked that she had never seen such a small airport, "with luggage coming out a hole in the cinderblock wall." Driving along the open road, we came upon a car overturned in the ditch. The wheels were still turning, so it had just happened. With nothing else but prairie in sight, we stopped to see if we could help. Luckily an ambulance soon arrived, but when they learned I was a nurse, they asked me to accompany the injured young woman in the ambulance to Valentine, Nebraska, fifty miles beyond our destination in Rosebud. Pam drove my car following the ambulance. Meanwhile, inside the ambulance the young woman about my age told me that she was in college, coming home for the weekend. With very little equipment inside, this ambulance was mostly just a ride. The girl had trauma of her head and arm that I could see, with possible internal injuries. She was becoming restless and combative on our ride, which could mean that her condition was getting worse. I was relieved when we finally arrived safely at the Valentine hospital. Pam met me there and we went home to Rosebud to start our fun visit. I later was glad to hear indirectly that the girl quickly healed and returned to college.

All my letters to Pam of the isolation and loneliness seemed less true with the recent addition of Lenel and Brad, but it was wonderful to have Pam with me again. She accompanied me to the Lakota music class and we learned the rabbit dance together. We explored the Badlands and she got a sense of the vast openness of this stark land. I had been telling her how the entertainment was limited to the Starlight movie theatre, 10 miles away in Mission. A ticket cost 50 cents and popcorn a dime. A good deal even for 1974, if you were working, which 70 percent of Rosebud was not. Pam liked the glowing stars on the ceiling. Nearby stood the other social outlet, the Western Bowl & Cafe, which served excellent chocolate cream pie accompanied by the clash of bowling pins. That and powwows were all the entertainment options we had found. We worked many extra shifts, and when we were off duty, our friends were usually working, so really even board games, cards or group activities were scarce. Judy and I had been so lonely at first that we actually had thrown all our silverware onto the floor one day, as we had heard that if you drop a fork it means company is coming.

Actually, I'd had one other brief visitor that spring, which created some talk. My friend Jim Moran, the campus priest from the University of Connecticut came to see firsthand what I'd been telling him in letters. We'd become friends as I'd sung in the folk mass there four times a week. Several of the older nurses were concerned that my apartment had only one bedroom (twin beds) and they were scandalized by their own speculation. But Jim was a good man of the cloth, and our most exciting part of the visit was when he cooked spaghetti carbonara for me, a recipe from his time spent in Rome. I still recall that rich smoky flavor. He stayed a few days seeing local sights and continued onward to a meeting somewhere.

Though we did not mix socially at the time, we later learned that the docs spent time playing cards and loading shotgun shells for hunting. Dr. Tosi was from back East too, and he had not done much hunting before coming to Rosebud. Once he went hunting with the other docs and shot an antelope. He says,

"I felt like l had shot my grandmother. The antelope tasted bad to me, but then I felt like I had to eat the whole thing too and not waste it."

Pam had laughed when I'd told her of the travelling salesman. One day before her visit as I was napping on my couch, I was startled by a rare knock at the door. I answered it to find a man selling pots and pans. Really? In Rosebud? Though I didn't need any pans, I was so lonely that I let him in to hear his sales pitch anyway, as a social diversion. The salesman gave his spiel for a couple of hours, and I made no attempt to shorten or stop it. This visitor was such a welcome diversion, which shows my isolation and desperate lack of social life. I even invested in an expensive set of stainless cookware, with a fifty-year warrantee. As a bonus, he also gave me a coffeepot and a set of knives, which I still use forty-some years later, so maybe I struck a good deal after all.

I suggested to Pam that she might like to take a walk around the rolling hills by the hospital while I was working. We had exhausted most of the other entertainment options. She set off by herself one sparkling brisk day. As she tells it,

"Because of my Italian olive skin and dark hair, which I sometimes wore in braids, I was occasionally mistaken for an Indian myself. Plus, I was wearing the beaded and rawhide wristband that Nancy had made for me in the Lakota style. As I climbed a hill, and approaching the crest, I felt the hairs rise on the back of my neck, feeling that someone was watching me. I looked around, and eventually saw on a distant ridge there were two Indians and one was pointing a rifle … at me. I had grown up on a farm with two brothers, and their guns, who occasionally used me for target practice, so I was attuned to the feeling of someone aiming at me. I knew this guy's gun and knew the distance, and thought, *He can't hit me.* I kept walking along my ridge, and they kept walking along theirs. Eventually our two ridges merged, and I saw that the rifleman was slightly younger than me, and quite good-looking. He was no longer aiming his rifle at me. I started talking to him, and we began walking together. He invited me to his house, one of the small shabby government houses, about the size of our chicken coop on the farm. He was well-read, and he started talking about books. Inside, I was impressed with his book collection, including many classics. I complimented his taste, and he said, "I could sell you some books."

"Since he had so recently been aiming his rifle at me, I thought I'd better not turn him down, risking an insult. So, I offered him five bucks and bought a couple of books. Although I never read them, I still have them today. I never saw him again, but the experience certainly added to the uniqueness of this Rosebud visit."

Pam is a sparkling friendly Italian with a ready smile who enjoys gathering a crowd of friends. One day she said,

"Let's have a party!"

I was dubious about who would come, but while the volunteers were there, we thought we could scrape together enough folks for a small gathering. I don't know who came up with the idea to have a fondue and wine tasting party on a dry reservation with rampant alcohol issues, but somehow, we thought it would be fun. We drove the 100 miles round trip to Valentine to get a fondue pot and our supplies. On Thursday Pam made a sign to put up in the hospital for the staff:

The Roses of Rosebud invite you to a Fondue and Wine Tasting.

When: Saturday night.   Where: my address.

We had fun making all the various foods to dip in multiple pots: oil for meat and savories, cheeses for bread, and several chocolate dips for fruits and sweets.

By then, after Judy had left I had moved to my third furnished Rosebud apartment, a five-minute walk down the lane from the hospital. This one-bedroom unit sat across the duplex's hall from Stephanie's apartment, so we planned to use both spaces for the party. We each had a generous living room space with a couch and adequate kitchen with laminate and chrome table and chairs. We had hoped for maybe a handful of guests, including the volunteers. Steph and I worked our hospital shift the previous night, slept a bit, and as evening approached we prepared frantically with Pam, Lenel, Brad, and Sue Beeson. Boy did it smell good as the cooks enjoyed a lot of quality control sampling.

We were almost ready when the doorbell rang and the first guests began to arrive. We didn't recognize anyone. They said they had seen the sign at the hospital. More and more strangers poured in, from as far away as Oklahoma, Utah, and Colorado! Most said they had never heard of fondue, some were curious to try it, but many just wanted the wine. As we recall, many had not brought anything to share, but the event resembled the Biblical loaves and fishes. We don't recall running out of food or drink, but we certainly had not prepared for the total of about 200 Cowboys and Indians that showed up at my place. The party went well into the wee hours, and a couple of guests even stayed overnight. The crowd mixed well and everyone seemed to have a good time, though we never saw most of them again. It was an epic event in a town with a population of 736. And Pam still knows how to throw a great party.

Pam had been brought up hearing that one would get into heaven if one saw their initials in the sky. After the loaves-and-fishes fondue and wine episode, she says she saw her initials in the sky as her plane took off to return home.   *Waunsilapi.*

19. Back porch sing-along with neighbors, Lenel and the author.

20. Chases Women Lake, where we tried to camp.

21. Lenel and Pam prepping for the fondue party.

13. Goodbye

RUTH. *WOWICAKE.* THAT WHICH IS REAL, THE WAY THE WORLD IS.

PERSEVERANCE. *WOWACINTANKA.* TO PERSIST, TO STRIVE IN SPITE OF DIFFICULTIES.

SACRIFICE. ICICUPI. TO GIVE OF ONESELF, AN OFFERING.

BRAVERY. WOOHITIKE. HAVING OR SHOWING COURAGE.

RESPECT. *WAWOOHOLA.* TO BE CONSIDERATE, TO HOLD IN HIGH ESTEEM.

HONOR. *WAYUONIHAN.* TO HAVE INTEGRITY, TO HAVE AN HONEST AND UPRIGHT CHARACTER.

GENEROSITY. *CANTEYUKE.* TO GIVE, TO SHARE, TO HAVE A HEART.

WISDOM. *WOKSAPE.* TO UNDERSTAND WHAT IS RIGHT AND TRUE, TO USE KNOWLEDGE WISELY.

HUMILITY. *UNSIICIYAPI.* TO BE HUMBLE, MODEST, UNPRETENTIOUS.

LOVE. *CANTOGNAKE.* TO PLACE AND HOLD IN ONE'S HEART.

FORTITUDE. *CANTEWASAKE.* STRENGTH OF HEART AND MIND.

COMPASSION. *WAUNSILAPI.* TO CARE, TO SYMPATHIZE.

lthough I had come to Rosebud with no plan for how long I would stay, by late summer of 1974 it had become clear that my time was coming to a close. My only brother planned to be married in October in Connecticut, and I wanted to be home to join in the fun. But that wasn't the main reason. While events at work kept life there overly full, my social life was generally nonexistent once the volunteers left, and I felt that part of me was withering up. In the summer of 1974, I was 23 years old and in my prime, but felt like I was in my eighties at times. When not working, I mostly slept, or sometimes I would visit my friends at the hospital who were working. I felt that there must be more to life than work and sleep. I wrestled greatly with my decision toward the end of the summer, as Rosebud and its people were so needy, and they had become such a part of me. It was ripping me apart to think of leaving.

I had been a suburban girl who had moved away to expand my world. I had found growth through my struggles with loneliness, with trying to turn work chaos into some semblance of organization, with embracing a new culture, and with being open to the possibilities of new experiences. I had made some connections and shared some discoveries. After my only visit home, I returned with a few photos of Connecticut. Some of my Rosebud friends were so surprised to see woods and fields of shade-grown tobacco fields under a sea of white nets. They had thought the whole area was a metropolis like New York City. They'd also been surprised at my relative lack of accent, expecting me to talk like a New Yorker or Bostonian. We'd all learned some things about each other.

I felt needed and fulfilled as a nurse. My organizational and care giving skills had developed tremendously. I was often in charge of the unit, and sometimes acted as supervisor of the hospital. My confidence had grown while my anxiety had abated. My co-workers had become comrades in the trenches, with many intense experiences as well as humor bonding us together. I had grown immensely as a person, embracing the reverence for nature and spirituality of the Sioux culture. I valued their strength of community, strong traditions and ceremonies tying them deeply to their home, their ancestors, and the land. I especially respected the perseverance and strength that it must have taken to hold onto those traditions through the oppression that these people had withstood. I had been able to break through some of the barriers of hostility and distrust to see the warmth and generosity of some of these people. But living with so much struggle, damage, desolation, and tragedy was taking its toll on me, even as an outsider. Unlike most of the Rosebud people who were trapped by poverty and traditional ties to their ancestors and to the land, I did have the option to leave.

Our first trailer home in Mission had been across from the grazing land of the tribal buffalo herd, with a view of the big prairie sky that went on for more than a hundred miles. I loved to watch the storms roll in or see how the sunsets took up the whole sky. I never would have seen these sights back in our woodsy area of Connecticut. One day Judy and I had been surprised to see a male buffalo lock horns with a longhorn bull and fight over a female buffalo. The buffalo butted the bull down and he didn't get up. We were worried, so we called the tribal police to get help for the animal. When the police came the bull got up, but when they left, the fight began again. We left them alone after that and went for a walk, figuring that they'd been doing their rituals for a long time without our interference.

Many patients had highlighted my time working in Rosebud. I had been challenged to work with older patients who spoke only Lakota and no English. Amelia He Dog, in her nineties, had a wonderful ancient face so brown and wrinkled exactly like the badlands, mirroring the land that had sustained her for all those years. Her bright eyes peered out from canyons of wrinkles, and she would offer a toothless smile in response to my gestures of communication. I regret that I never got the chance or took the opportunity to speak with her through an interpreter during our hectic days. I do remember that Lorna Her Many Horses and the other Lakota staff acknowledged her age and held her life experience in great esteem.

Dr. Tosi had another experience with an ancient one. He needed to obtain her medical history, so he did work with an interpreter. He learned that Maggie Little Dog was ninety-two years old and had been at the original Wounded Knee Massacre in 1890. She remembered hiding in a ditch when she was ten years old with Chief Bigfoot who was dying of TB. They hid by piling brush over themselves while witnessing the chaos, dust, and screams of the massacre all around them. Dr. Tosi points out that this remarkable woman had survived from the Stone Age to the Space Age of the 1970s.

I remember a man who had lost his vision and both legs to diabetes. He wouldn't allow me to care for him in the hospital after his second amputation. Although he could not see me, he knew I was white. No matter what I said to him or how much he needed help, he stood firm in his convictions, even though he went home unable physically to stand at all.

Norman Short Bull was one of the first patients to receive care in our brand-new ICU. Some electricians had come from Iowa, an event in itself, to rewire the old four-bed ward by the nurses' station and to move the old EKG monitors from the maternity hall into the big room. After the nurses took a brief class in cardiac care we were good to go. Norman Short Bull was in his forties, and he had suffered a very severe heart attack. He remained delirious for several days as his heart tried to get enough oxygen to his brain, and I was taking care of him through his difficult illness. When he finally became coherent, I learned that he was a very pleasant man and we enjoyed some good conversations together. He eventually recovered and arrived at the hospital several weeks later looking for me. He had made me a gift, his remarkable drawing of a woman's face resembling mine, with a feather headband. I still treasure this portrait, and the memory of this gentle gifted man. He died a few months later, ironically choking on a chicken bone in a busy restaurant in the metropolis of Rapid City.

Quannah Crow Dog, the baby I had transported on my first day of work, later came back to our pediatrics unit. I remarked to another nurse how sweet Quannah was, compared to his ill-tempered father Leonard Crow Dog, who had threatened to kill me if his baby had not survived the early illness. I was mortified to realize that Quannah's mother was standing behind me when I made my comment. Perhaps either I apologized, or she pretended not to hear, or possibly she agreed with me, as I don't recall any big scene there. Leonard Crow Dog was an AIM warrior but also a spiritual healer whose intimidating presence cast a wide shadow for us.

Ollie Pretty Bird was a wonderful outpatient aide who had been teaching me how to do beadwork in return for lessons in knitting and crochet. I definitely got the better end of that deal in terms of expertise, but we each started the other with new skills. It had taken some effort to break through her very reserved nature, and when she heard that I had decided to leave, she said, "Oh, Nancy, not you too." Ollie had invested her trust in me, and her words showed me that my leaving felt like a betrayal to her. It still hurts. I had given so much of myself in Rosebud, but I always felt that I took away so much more than I gave.

I arrived at Rosebud in August of 1973 and stayed into September of 1974. As I finalized my plans to leave, I had a sudden intense sensation of dwelling in the here and now. My focus on the present sharpened, which was a concept usually fleeting in my life. I had been used to viewing my life as leading up to and looking back on experiences. Considering the present was a very liberating feeling. I could see the whole composition of my past encompassing my present identity, and a completely blank future—anything goes!

My friend Pam generously flew back in from Connecticut to share the return drive with me in Shigella. The Rosebud tribe gave me a lovely pair of locally made ochre and blue pottery vases as a going-away gift. My last vision as we drove off into the golden sunrise was of my friend Rose, newly promoted to night supervisor. She waved from the hospital doorway, and then disappeared down the hallway chasing bats with an upraised broom. In my heart, I knew that my time at Rosebud truly would remain in my memory as *Magic and Tragic*.

Wowicake.
Wowacintanka.
Icicupi.
Woohitike.
Wawoohola.
Wayuonihan.
Canteyuke.
Woksape.
Unsüciyapi.
Cantognake.
Cantewasake.
Waunsilapi.

22. Sue and Rose hunting for ghosts.

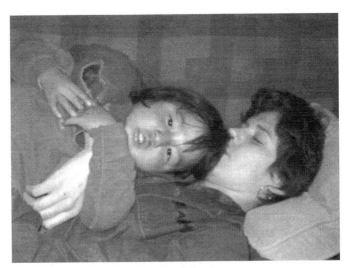

23. Sue and Freddie.

24. Rosebud pottery vase from the tribe, Richard Fool Bull's courting flute and portrait by Norman Short Bull.

25. Yellow necklace made by Wanda's brother, earrings and spiral necklace that Ollie taught me to make.

The Present – Rosebud Revisited

26. The new Rosebud PHS turtle-shaped hospital.

14. Rosebud update 2016

Rosebud's health care in the twenty-first century bears an uncanny resemblance to the time I was there in 1973-4. Actually, in many ways it's even worse now.

Sometime after we left Rosebud, the Public Health Service tried to give the old condemned hospital building to the tribe, but they were wise to refuse. A new PHS hospital in the shape of a turtle, to symbolize long life and good health was built and dedicated in 1989. A physical therapy department and a dialysis center are now part of the health system. The policy is to hire Indians first, but with limited education opportunities the challenge remains to find qualified staff. Paired with the chronic lack of funding and remote location, at various times entire units of this newer hospital remain closed.

In December 2015 the Rosebud emergency room was closed by federal inspectors due to substandard care. Employees were hand-washing surgical instruments for six months while the sterilizer was broken. One woman had waited forty-five minutes before being evaluated for a heart attack. Another had delivered a baby prematurely on the bathroom floor. But by closing this remote facility in rural South Dakota, all the patients were now condemned to delaying their care. They would all have to make their way an additional forty to fifty miles to the nearest hospitals in Valentine, Nebraska and Winner, South Dakota. This included critically bleeding trauma patients, those with breathing problems, and mothers in labor. Each minute counts in these emergencies. One has to wonder about the cost in lives lost. Two other hospitals in the Indian Health Service Great Plains area were also ordered to cut services. Wikipedia sources report that during the time that Rosebud's ER was closed, five babies were born in ambulances and nine people died on that fifty-mile stretch to the nearest hospital.

We would be outraged here in Maryland, even with several other local hospitals available, and the media would be all over the story. But in this forgotten pocket of our country with no safety net, the situation is barely a blip on our radar here near our nation's capital.

Remarkably, I discovered this piece of news as I was researching statistics for this memoir. I happened to come upon a news release from the National Indian Health Board. In February 2016 the U.S.

Senate held a hearing about the "substandard quality of care" of three Indian Health Service hospitals, including Rosebud. A plan was being developed to address the problems, but meanwhile precious time was lost while the ER remained closed and other problems continued. This report states that the Indian Health Service has been underfunded since it was founded in 1955, with less than half of the funding per person than for other Americans. The unfilled doctor positions average thirty-seven percent. How could care not be below standard? It's a very different world from where the bureaucrats live, with their premium health care. People in Rosebud continue to be victimized by a system meant to serve them. Rosebud illuminates the injustice and highlights the vast challenges and difference in life here compared to many other areas of our country.

The emergency room crisis had been haunting me, as I remembered how much people depended on the facility, such as it was, even when I was there. I've been carrying the people of Rosebud in my heart ever since, and especially this past couple of years as I'd been writing of these eventful memories. Since reading the press release I'd been trying to get more information, to clarify the situation and to advocate for improvements. I'd read conflicting reports, and information was sparse. Multiple calls and letters to various parties in the Indian Health Service, National Indian Health Board, and tribal offices had yielded very little response. I was told in March by a representative of the NIHB that "We will be forming task forces. We're taking it slow and doing it right this time." But three months later the ER doors remained closed and even the task forces had yet to be formed. Taking it slow indeed.

In April 2016, three of the nurses who had worked with me at Rosebud—my "Rosebuddies"—reunited for the first time. Stephanie, Judy, and Rose were all willing to join me in meeting with an Indian Health Service representative or anyone involved in the situation. But despite trying several avenues I could find no one to meet with us. Maybe we just hadn't found the right doors to knock on.

Whether from apathy or overwork or something else, I saw the lack of response as yet another symptom of the problems of bureaucracy imposed on Rosebud. I was appalled and frustrated. I wanted to help. The Rosebuddies told me that maybe writing and sharing this book was enough and now it could be someone else's turn. Maybe. I still had a few ideas.

On May 2, 2016 the Washington *Post* buried a short item partway down a page in the middle of a section: "Two reservation hospitals agree to changes." Changes included the appointment of a monitor to provide periodic progress reports, and the privatization of the facilities' emergency rooms. I felt like I'd been holding my breath while waiting for news about Rosebud's ER. With this article, I was now able to exhale, five months later. I still wondered when the ER would reopen and how the privatization might change things. Cautiously optimistic, I hoped to find out more when Steph and I planned to revisit Rosebud in September. Maybe someone would talk with us then.

An online *Argus Leader* item on June 13, 2016, noted that in Rosebud an embattled hospital announced the shuttering of additional departments following the death of a staff member who was a key clinician. Surgical and OB patients were to be diverted to Valentine, Martin, and Winner (44-55 miles). Urgent care, outpatient and inpatient services remained available. Private contractors were staffing the ER and the hospital was seeking other services.

An August 2016 press release from the National Indian Health Board stated:

"Tribal Consultation with the National Indian Health Board and a mobile senate interest group in Rapid City, SD. will be necessary to achieve the full potential [that] legislation can have on erasing the health disparities experienced in Tribal communities. A pressing need and opportunity exists within the Indian Health Service for structural reform. Attention must be directed at improving the quality of care at federally run IHS facilities by strengthening agency-wide standards for hiring, management, and delivery of care. The IHS, and other related agencies within the HHS, must employ all tools at their disposal to recruit and retain qualified, culturally competent health professionals. Training must be provided in Tribal communities to improve health and medical literacy."

Although these important issues were still being debated, this article didn't appear to reflect any specific action plan. At least the talk hadn't faded away at this point.

In an April 2013 blog on Stanford Medical's site, medical student L. Lamsam recounts his brief time shadowing a doctor at Rosebud hospital. He was impressed with the breadth and scope of the physician's job "like the cowboys of medicine." One doc was covering the outpatient clinic, the inpatient medical floor, the ER, and assisting in the operating room. It sounds like not much has changed from the 70s in that regard. He writes of outdated equipment that staff had to "MacGyver" (creatively piece together) to perform a function. That sounds familiar too. He speaks of remarkable results considering the limited resources and the complexity of the patients. "Poor equipment, an overload of seriously ill patients, and lack of access to a higher level of care demanded that the already short-staffed IHS doctors go above and beyond what is normally required." Interestingly, this student saw Rosebud as a "world-class training resource and a great lesson in how to do more with less," especially in these increasingly budget-conscious times.

I feel the need to include some additional information relating to Rosebud's quality of life. My purpose is not to expose the pain for someone else's entertainment, but to build a case for action and improvement of these conditions.

Rosebud in Todd County has long been and remains the second poorest county of the U.S., following only the Pine Ridge reservation which continues to hold that dubious distinction. In a 2013 tribal education report, only fifty-six percent of the people had public high school diplomas. Less than twelve percent of these finish college, though more have completed some college studies. A few professional physicians, lawyers, and teachers have returned to the reservation to give back and help support their community.

According to 2012 government statistics, Rosebud's unemployment remains at about seventy to eighty percent, due largely to lack of opportunity. Seventy-six percent of those few who are employed live below poverty level. Employers consist mainly of farms or ranches, federal, local and tribal governments, and health or education facilities. Twenty-nine percent of the people are homeless, and fifty-nine percent live in sub-standard housing. Families are known to crowd together in order to shelter needy members and many take-in elderly relatives.

The Rosebud Sioux Tribe has also followed the Native American trend to build a casino. However, because of its remote location it is not nearly as profitable as many of its counterparts. We hope to learn more about this firsthand too.

"Tribes like the Sioux that followed the buffalo lost both their way of life and their food source due to western expansion. Forced to live on the most desolate land and to turn to unfamiliar farming lifestyles, they were left with food from the government's commodity program—flour, pasta, rice, peanut butter, canned food, cheese—a diet distributed from warehouses on the reservation, devoid of fresh food. Today, it's still nearly impossible to find fresh fruit and vegetables on the Rosebud Reservation" as stated in the Fall 2013 *Stanford Medical Magazine.*

In May of 2017, the Washington *Post* reported that the average U.S. life expectancy is now seventy-eight years. Some areas of Colorado boast a rate as high as eighty-five years. However, in Rosebud and Pine Ridge the average lifespan is only sixty-seven years for babies born in 2017. A Stanford Medical blog from April 2013, found that on average Rosebud men could expect to live to age forty-seven, compared with a U.S. average of seventy-seven. Even Haiti's average was found to be higher at forty-eight. A "health disadvantage" is cited in these areas, with "diseases of despair" including smoking, physical inactivity, obesity, and high blood pressure. Not mentioned are alcohol and drug dependence, but these are commonly associated with pockets of poverty as well. All of these are preventable, in theory. Lifestyle behaviors are not only causes of these conditions but are also symptoms of the disadvantage related to decades of policy decisions. Poverty is part of the toxic brew of substance dependence, dysfunctional families, and educational failures. These are repeated generation after generation, according to the New York *Times*, May 9, 2012. In Rosebud, diabetes, suicide, and substance abuse are epidemic.

Alcoholism was an overwhelming problem when we worked at the hospital. While this remains a huge challenge, now substance abuse has taken an additional form. With more than sixty percent of Rosebud's population using methamphetamines, this tsunami is overwhelming the limited resources even further. An article by M. Pember in the May 2016 online issue of *Indian Country Today* details the situation. The meth problem began before 2005 and comes in waves. Some of these waves are especially deadly with strong, cheap, and readily available meth tied to organized crime. The DEA reported that drug cases had increased seven-fold from 2009-2014, with the reservation crime rate five times the national average. At least forty percent of the crime was directly related to meth, especially burglaries, domestic violence and assaults.

Rosebud's correctional officers are further challenged by a lack of training for meth detox, which is unpredictable, and dangerously violent. Acute withdrawal averages up to three months, often followed by suicidal behaviors. Meth addicts may become physically ill too, but hospitalization is not an option due to their sudden and strong violent outbursts, so they remain in the corrections facility, at times restrained in a chair for periods of hours. Counselors from the tribal Drug and Alcohol Treatment Center offer recovery classes at the jail. In 2010 The Rosebud Sioux Tribe (RST) opened the first meth-specific treatment facility in Indian country. Although the 5-year funding ended, the program continues with a skeleton staff. Participation is court-ordered for a forty-eight-week program, with the first three months taking place in jail. Director Ed Purcell states, "All treatment is 100% successful, even if the client does not have a favorable outcome. The intervention changes how they view themselves in the relationship with drugs. One client told me I'd taken all the fun out of using—he kept hearing my voice in his head and it spoiled his high." The national cure rate is less than ten percent. The Youth and Family Services organization holds public awareness trainings and works with Mothers Against Meth.

Researchers have found in recent years that intergenerational trauma, or pain experienced by earlier generations can be inherited and can influence even the structure and expression of germline genes, a process known as imprinting. These genetic changes can be passed down for generations. Intergenerational trauma such as the Indian boarding schools, war or holocaust makes genes more likely to respond negatively to stress and trauma. The trauma can trigger behaviors such as alcoholism, domestic and sexual abuse, resulting in more cycles of trauma and more antisocial responses. With Indian children torn from their families and hearing messages of racial and cultural inferiority in the boarding schools, several generations were created who have no concept of parenting or family life.

Some people, however, seem to have more resilience than others. This ability to cope can be encouraged by opportunities for self-discovery, taking care of oneself, finding family support, meditation and spiritual practices. Todd County High School classes from Mission have gone back to visit the infamous Carlisle boarding school in Pennsylvania to research and honor the names they found. Their families have said that you can feel the hurt they brought back with them. But in discovering and honoring a part of their past, they are also building strength and resilience.

Many of the people of Rosebud are understandably disillusioned with politics and tend to stay under the radar. However, much of the Native population is finding its voice in regard to climate issues and a rising tide of spirituality and traditions. Some younger people are learning how to live the old ways, again finding the strength of their ancestors. Social media now offers opportunities for many to connect from remote areas, though not everyone has this access yet. Native traditions embrace the concept of being Caretakers of Mother Earth. Spiritual ceremonies include the phrase, "All my relatives," including two-leggeds, four-leggeds, the flying creatures, swimmers, plants, rocks, and the earth itself. Many Natives including some people from Rosebud have become leaders in protecting water and land from industrial pollution and climate change, partnering with larger powerful organizations. The partnerships not only magnify their voices and efforts, but they may provide some legal defense in the court battles.

Despite all of its challenges, a lot of people choose to live on the reservation to be close to family, culture, and history. Stanford researchers found Rosebud to be "a close-knit community in a reservation that has survived a tragic history. There is a sense of pride and determination among those struggling against hopelessness that has taken so many young lives. Practicing the old ways resonates with an increased community pride and the strength of the ancestors is helping to wean some from their addictions."

In an article in the Fall 2013 *Stanford Medical Journal* entitled "Almost Without Hope: Seeking a Path to Health on the Rosebud Indian Reservation" psychologist Rebecca Foster spoke of her decision to get an education and return to help her people. "There is a difference between having to stay here because you are trapped and choosing to be here. One's a prison, the other is a home because you have something to give." She finds positive and wonderful things on the reservation including the strength of the community ties and connections with ceremonies and traditions.

A May 2017 article in *Indian Country Today* notes some signs of progress in the fight against diabetes. The incidence here is still twice that of whites, and those aged under eighteen are nine times as likely to develop Type II diabetes. Rosebud has a new mobile health unit to check on folks living in small remote communities. An annual Walk for Diabetes is raising awareness and offering support. A small Native youth camp is now being offered in the Southwest to teach diabetes prevention by encouraging good nutrition, exercise, and healthy lifestyle choices. Youth are reportedly enthusiastic learners, and they are bringing the prevention ideas home to their families.

In an episode of the CNN series *United Shades of America*, which aired on May 14, 2017, W. Kamau Bell visited the Sacred Stone water protectors' camp at Standing Rock, North Dakota, and the Pine Ridge reservations in South Dakota, which borders Rosebud. He found a lot of good happening there. Organizing in opposition to the pipeline activity has made a positive difference. The people are finding strength in practicing, teaching, and sharing their traditions. People are uniting toward a common goal in protecting the water and the earth. A moment is being seized and many people are again proud to be Native American. The traditional Lakota society recognized kinship through the mothers, and women are again assuming leadership roles. The challenges are certainly staggering, but Mr. Bell also found a surprising helping of joy, generosity, and laughter among the people he met. As many others have found, a sense of humor along with community spirit can work wonders to ease life's burdens. The words of these Lakota people echo and reverberate: "We are still here. We are the descendants of our strongest ancestors. Our hope and dignity are unconquerable."

15. Return to Rosebud 2016

Sometimes life carries you on a journey. I decided to return to Rosebud to gather more material for the book. I wanted to find out what was going on with the hospital and the ER situation, and to update my impressions of life in Rosebud. I also was hoping to get family contacts for permission to use names and photos. Another goal of this trip was to visit North Dakota, the last of the 50 U.S. states I had begun to explore when I first went to Rosebud with Judy in 1973.

Stephanie decided to join me this time, for support and company as well as her curiosity about what we would find in Rosebud now. Steph's curls remain her defining feature, now silver to match her wire rim glasses. She has worked to find a layer of peace in her life to blanket her nervous energy. Sharing tastes, values, and rhythms after all these years, we travel well together. Besides, she'd never been to North Dakota either, and we figured we'd never be closer.

THURSDAY, 9/8/16, MARYLAND TO NORTH DAKOTA.

The landscape on the connecting flight from Colorado to North Dakota mesmerized me, appearing as modern art. Tan and dusky patchwork squares with green irrigation circles were sparsely lined by long straight roads, like a Jean Miro painting. The lush dark of the Black Hills rose and became the irregular grayish clay Badlands. The dry scenery featured blue and silver ribbons of rivers and feathery branches of canyons, with indigo dots of lakes. We flew over the Missouri River, which appeared wider here than I'd expected. I looked for but did not see the Sacred Stone Camp gathering of several hundred bands of Indians and allies who were obstructing the Dakota Access Oil Pipeline (DAPL) project to protect the water supply.

We finally set foot in North Dakota. While Steph went to rent the car at the Bismarck airport, I spotted a small cluster of Indians in their twenties, one with a feather in his hat. I asked if they were heading to the pipeline site. They looked surprised and replied yes. I told them I'd been following the events in the Lakota Times, which also registered surprise. I guess they didn't expect this from a silver-haired white Eastern lady. I asked if I could donate some money, which surprised them more. The guy in the hat introduced himself. "My name is Lehigh and we are Navajo coming in to join the camp." We shook hands and I thanked them for their efforts. I told them I'd continue sharing the Lakota Times posts with my Facebook friends, who were also sharing to get the word out, since there was sparse national media coverage. I mentioned my time in Rosebud and my memoir project, and I wished them good luck. This experience touched me deeply.

Steph returned with a cherry red Chevy Cruze, very similar in size and color to the Vega she'd had in Rosebud when we were buried in the blizzard. We headed out on route 1089 N, the same road that was blocked off about a hundred miles away for the pipeline camp. Because of the airline's schedule changes, we now didn't have time to go there. We hadn't allowed enough leeway in our schedule, and we only had a few days in Rosebud as it was. Regretfully, it just wasn't the right time for us.

We headed west, as the green hills and patchy clouds stunned us with their vast beauty, in contrast to the close woodland and urban landscapes back home. Over the next hundred miles the clouds gathered and darkened. Holes of light created bright areas of fascination. The hills gentled into rolling plains, still greener than we'd expected. A few small groups of cattle dotted the hills. We passed "the biggest cow in the world" sculpture profiled on a hillside. Several small refineries appeared, one with huge piles of stacked pipe near a Missouri River bridge. A few scattered small black oil wells pumped steadily. An extensive wind farm rotated in the distance. Large sunflower fields past their prime wore seed heads aging on their stalks. We passed a few smaller cornfields, some dried for the season. But the sky was the main event, as the sun lowered and began to gild the grass, glowing peach on the horizon between dark rain clouds. A few sudden showers blinded us and cleared just as quickly. As we came to the Teddy Roosevelt National Park Badlands, a bright rainbow popped out on the right. I was feeling nervous about how we would be received in Rosebud this time and hoped this was a good sign.

Steph and I talked about how grateful we were to witness this amazing sky display and the circumstances that had led us here to this place and time—rental car challenges, flight schedule changes, and many other factors, old and new.

In the quaint touristy town of Medora, we found our Badlands Motel snuggled beside a jagged clay cliff with a stunning view outside our door. So far, expectations exceeded.

FRIDAY, 9/9/16, TEDDY ROOSEVELT NATIONAL PARK IN MEDORA, NORTH DAKOTA.

I awakened thinking about the name dilemma for the Rosebud book. I had modified and printed a permission form to use peoples' names, but I wasn't sure how valid it would be without a publisher on board yet. Just before we'd left for the Dakotas I'd consulted my friend Pat's husband, a publishing lawyer. He told me that the forms are state-specific depending on the location of the publisher, plus in this case tribal law may also be a factor. Also, after forty years many of my "characters" have died. How does one designate a family representative? What if family members disagree about granting permission?

My goals for this Rosebud visit were to make contacts, ask questions, maybe start a buzz about the book, and to let folks know that the proceeds will be returned to the community. If I could untangle the name hairball, I might return again to get the permits once I had a publisher. It was suggested that I try to hire a student to do this, but it seemed appropriate to do it in person, plus I'd be interested in meeting the families myself. I could explain more in person and field questions. IF anyone in Rosebud would talk with me at all. It was a hostile place when we'd lived there. I planned to start looking for a publisher when we got back. At least the memoir part was now recorded on paper to share with friends and family, even if the stories got no wider audience.

We stepped out the motel door to a beautiful clear morning in the low 50s. I was so excited to finally go see Teddy Roosevelt National Park. Stephanie's one wish was to see a bison sometime on this trip.

We enjoyed a wonderful breakfast at the Rough Rider Hotel with Teddy Roosevelt's family portrait watching over our booth, joining us for our meal. We had remembered Dakota food as pretty basic, so this breakfast was a pleasant surprise. Steph savored her order of sweet potato pancakes with blueberries and I was wowed by ricotta-lemon flapjacks with a generous load of fresh mixed berries. The hot coffee's aroma and fresh taste gave us a delightful start to our chilly day.

On to the park to get our Golden Eagle passes, for free lifetime entry to all national parks. We took five hours to navigate the 35-mile scenic loop drive, as we kept stopping to savor the breathtaking scenery. Several prairie dog towns charmed us with their critters' chirping barks, wagging tails, digging, standing, jumping, and scurrying behaviors. The park ranger later told us that prairie dogs have a very developed language, with different vocalizations for *hawk, coyote, other thing that flies—not hawk,* and they can recognize specific people.

We saw feral horses, and then we spotted a bison on a far hill. Stephanie was thrilled. Our second objective met, after reaching North Dakota. Later another bison appeared about twenty yards away. We watched for a long time as he calmly grazed, feeling very privileged to see him so close. A few miles later we stopped behind a car to see two huge bison right across the road. I got out to take some pictures, careful not to approach them as we'd been warned how dangerous and unpredictable these two thousand- pound animals can be, sprinting up to 30 mph. One calmly ambled closer and crossed the road right in front of me. Steph was becoming agitated, urgently calling to me to get back in the car. I wasn't worried about the bison though. He was calm, and I hadn't approached him. He had come to me, amazingly. But once the car was no longer between us, I quietly got back inside for a buffer zone. I could hear him breathing and chewing right beside my window as he grazed! I could have touched his thick brown wooly coat, but I didn't. So magnificent. An honor to be so close. We were breathless and humbled and so grateful. We waited about twenty minutes until the two huge creatures meandered away. Farther on, a few cars lined up to watch a small herd of bison making their way across the road. The longer we watched, the more bison appeared from the grassy hills and gullies, about a hundred total, of all ages. We saw light tan newborns, older darker calves still nursing, entire families, with the Grand Poohbah silently watching over the herd from a nearby hillside. I could hear a few of them softly lowing as they grazed, as if saying, "Mmm mm good." We watched for a long time, as the herd gently gathered, surrounding us. Elated and completely blown away, I hoped this was another good omen for the Rosebud visit, as bison are sacred to the Lakota people.

We stopped for a late lunch at Medora's Little Missouri Saloon, which sported revolvers and rifles as doorknobs. It smelled of stale beer but the folks were friendly and the taco salad was tasty. At another section of the park, the Painted Canyon Overlook offered panoramic views too vast for the camera, but of course we tried to capture the moment and practice our selfie skills. More bison by the parking lot here.

We returned to the motel to call home and recall the gifts of our amazing day. A sign was posted for a hot air balloon festival the following day.

SATURDAY, 9/10/16, MEDORA, NORTH DAKOTA, TO BLACK HILLS, SOUTH DAKOTA.

At 9:30 am, already we'd had a remarkable day. Up at dawn for a balloon ascension right outside our door by the motel parking lot. Eight huge colorful balloons filled with hot air as we watched and shivered, holding paper coffee cups to warm our hands in the frosty morning. We thought of the folks back home in Maryland in the hundred-degree heat wave as we noticed the frost on the motel roof. As the massive balloons slowly inflated, they rotated from side-lying to upright positions. A burly bearded man resembling the Wizard of Oz climbed into the nearest basket and turned on the burner below the rainbow striped fabric with a whoosh. In a short time, the tethers were freed and it began to drift aloft, rising from the cliff's shadow into the dawn, amplifying its bright colors. One by one, each balloon slowly rose and gently disappeared over the cliff, silently floating above the National Park's badlands, bison and prairie dogs.

Steph and I proceeded to enjoy another lovely breakfast at Rough Riders: apple caramel raisin bread pudding with egg, bacon, and blessed hot coffee by the fireplace. Such a pleasant surprise, as we had been expecting to eat truck stop food in the Dakotas all week.

We found an open bookshop at 9am, The Amble Inn, with a wonderful collection including Western books. Steph bought one about Leonard Crow Dog, the Rosebud medicine man who had once threatened my life. I chose *The Lakota Way* by Joseph Marshall from Rosebud, hoping it would center and strengthen me for my anticipated encounters in Rosebud. We chatted with the owner, and he asked me to let him know when my book is available. Balloon launch and book interest—a fine send-off from North Dakota.

We headed next for the Black Hills of South Dakota. Turning south we found ourselves in a National Grasslands area, comparable to National Forests back East, except with grass instead of trees. Some small farms and fields, with a few scattered Black Angus cattle punctuating the area, but mostly very brown and stark, like how we'd remembered Rosebud. We passed through the town of Amadon, about 5 houses and an empty post office. We did see a police car parked at the roadside with a decaying dummy at the wheel to monitor traffic.

A few buttes and mesas began to appear out of the rolling hills. My first wild badger sighting, but alas it was roadkill. We entered South Dakota with little fanfare, missing a photo op of the small welcome sign as Steph drove the speed limit of 80 mph on this straight two-lane country road. I kept trying to imagine this vast land without the barbed wire fences, utility lines, cultivated fields, and cell towers, back when everything roamed freely. But this land is probably about as open as it gets anymore in these modern times.

Two tiny buildings emerged on the horizon, with a sign as we approached telling us we had arrived in Crow Butte. We stopped at the Mercantile, with an abandoned-looking City Hall next door. Not another building on the vast open horizon. We were hoping for directions to the geographic center of the U.S. that we'd seen on the map. But the lady said, "They moved it cuz it was on private land. You can see the monument 'bout 25 miles south now in Belle Fourche." I thanked her and bought some elk and bison jerky for gifts, plus a postcard of a windmill farm at the U.S. Capitol and some car snacks.

As we pulled back onto 85 South and got up to speed, we saw elk and then a few antelope, common here but not in Maryland. When we spotted an enormous herd in the distance, we slowed for a look with my binoculars. I focused, paused and handed the binocs to Steph. We burst out laughing. The magnificent multitude turned out to be hay rolls! But really, the previous ones had definitely been moving animals with legs and white rumps, some with horns.

The Black Hills began to rise up a deep purple color on the horizon, contrasting with the tan grasslands. An impressive sight as one can begin to appreciate their sacredness to the Lakota people. We continued into the scenic Spearfish Canyon. Towering dark evergreens and brilliant yellow aspens, with jagged rock cliffs in shades of gold and buff veined with dark shadows. Farther south, darker cliffs with rushing sparkling creeks and azure lakes appeared from among the dark and golden trees. The temperature dropped from 80 degrees on the prairie to 68 in the hills, and into the 50s later at dinnertime. As the shadows lengthened, we stopped in Hill City, scoring the last motel room in town.

SUNDAY, 9/11/16, BLACK HILLS TO ROSEBUD.

Over breakfast, big news from the DAPL pipeline and Sacred Stone Camp dominated the front page and first section of the Sunday Rapid City *Journal.* In the 1970s when we were last there, Rapid City was not known to be sympathetic to Indians, so this event seemed especially remarkable to us. A federal judge had ordered the pipeline work to resume, but this was immediately answered by a joint statement from the Departments of the Army, Justice, and the Interior. "Construction will not be allowed to proceed until environmental and cultural concern can be more fully addressed." A historic victory for the Indians, at least for now. And maybe a good omen for the Rosebud visit.

Stephanie had wanted to see the Crazy Horse monument near Mt. Rushmore today until she looked at the tourist brochure in the hotel lobby. After decades of construction, the monument itself still remains incomplete, but the site does feature high admission fees and a village of tourist shops. She was no longer interested.

We cranked up the music on Pandora whenever we could get a signal, singing along to the 70s music from our previous time in South Dakota: John Denver, Jim Croce, Simon & Garfunkel, James Taylor. Native flute music matched our quieter moods.

Highway 18 East brought us out of the hills to the extensive Pine Ridge Reservation. We saw a few tipis and frames, along with lots of mobile homes and junked cars. A small group of pinto and roan horses on a nearby ridge had graceful manes blowing in the prairie wind, as though posing for the similar logo of their well-advertised Prairie Winds Casino.

When we stopped to pay our respects at Wounded Knee, we found it essentially unchanged from our memories. The large sign stood at the roadside to commemorate the original massacre. Behind it we found six weathered picnic tables in a semicircle. An old bower of raw wooden trunks and crossbeams, with dead pine boughs falling to the tables offered little shelter from the sun, with the temperature hitting 92 even now in September. At one table sat a young man with an older woman. Another man approached us as we stood reading the memorial sign. He was selling beadwork and dreamcatchers, made by his uncle. He said he needed money to pay a utility bill, and he mentioned the 80 percent unemployment rate in the area. As I went back to the car for money to buy his uniquely sculpted dreamcatcher, the young man from the picnic table approached us. He said he represented a group of historians and keepers of the monument, wearing an official looking T-shirt. He invited us to come to their table with his auntie to learn about the 1973 Wounded Knee takeover. I replied that we had been around in 1973, but that I would like to learn more from them. He told us that the other man should not be selling anything in front of the sign, but that he should stay back at the tables. I'd already promised to buy something from the other man, and I suggested the T-shirt guy tell him and not me about the boundaries. As he returned to his table looking exasperated, another woman arrived selling beadwork in front of the sign, and a second car of tourists pulled up. We paid for our treasures as the seller said not to give the historian any money as he would gamble it away at the casino. He pointed to an eagle soaring overhead. Maybe we made the right decision?

Crossing the sparsely traveled main road we climbed the dirt path to the Wounded Knee cemetery, with the distinctive red and white striped archway. Inside the gate a Swedish flag caught my eye on a nearby grave, as if waiting for me with my Swedish heritage. I wondered about the connection on this grave marked Elk, but it remains a mystery to me. Other graves that caught my eye were Two Two, Red Cloud, and Respects Nothing. I picked a wildflower and some sage to twine into the chain link fence, adding it to the offerings of prayer ribbons, tobacco bundles, feathers, plastic flowers, cedar smudge sticks, and sage bundles. The constant prairie wind continued forming insistent waves in the parched prairie grasses and blowing our hair, as it always does here. From the obelisk monument at the cemetery's crest one can appreciate that there really was nowhere to run and hide from the massacre, with very few ponderosa pine trees among the shallow hills and gullies.

Another twenty-something guy with glazed eyes and a doughy face lurked inside the cemetery seeking donations for his drumming group, whose name was written on a wrinkled scrap of notebook paper in his hand. I tried to slip out while he was talking to other visitors, but he caught up to me, and I gave him a couple of bucks. I told him to keep drumming, as I recalled the power of the beat at the pow wow. He asked my name and told me his. I said we'd lived and worked in Rosebud. He replied, "We (Pine Ridge Oglala Sioux) don't get along with them (Rosebud Brule Sioux)." Then he asked for my cell phone number. I laughed and said, "You've got to be kidding!" He smiled. My steps crunched downhill back to the car. I did not make it to the history picnic table with the T-shirt guy and his auntie. It was all too weird. This solemn historic place deserves a proper visitor center, with paid Lakota educational workers and a fair-trade place to sell their crafts.

Back on the road, Highway 18 was a mess. Sporadic miles of construction, with signs for bumps out of sync with bumps which then pop up unexpectedly. Why not finish one segment rather than keeping the whole thing torn up? Because they can? Third world still. Will this continue into the winter blizzard season?

The sight of crops on the reservation looked novel and encouraging to us, though historically the Lakota people proudly followed the buffalo and when confined to reservations they resented and resisted the pressure to become farmers. Now, whether the tribe grew their own crops or leased the land, productive land was income for these desperately poor folks living in the poorest county in America. We passed sunflowers, corn fields and then an actual produce stand in the town of Bates, population 108. We entered the town of Swett with no population listed, which included a closed tavern and a building with a used car sign but no cars. Other sizable active communities had no name signs.

Reaching the Rosebud border at 3 p.m., we entered the Central Standard Time zone. Seeing that Rosebud sign gave us an almost surreal feeling. Looking beyond it to the vast open expanse of rolling prairie, we validated, "Yup. Still nothing there." I strained this time to appreciate the beauty that I had long ago discovered beyond the apparent emptiness. We embraced the open land itself, the unobstructed sky, and eventually the landscape gave us a few glades of trees and ponds. Probably more beauty would be found if we stepped outside of our travelling car.

One of the first structures we saw west of the once-familiar town of Mission was surrounded by barbed wire, with a tower and a couple of brick buildings. This criminal justice center had replaced the old jail, "Heartbreak Hotel" and blood bank in 2013. Some occasional solar panels and wind turbines in the landscape surprised and heartened us. Although it had been a long ride today, we decided to do a quick drive-through of the area before we tried to talk to folks tomorrow when businesses would open.

The Western Bowl and Café had morphed into the Boys and Girls Club with an impressive mural and skateboard ramp outside. We saw an updated high school with playing fields and kids out on the basketball courts. The old jail still stood on the main street, boarded up now, the "Heartbreak Hotel" sign no longer legible. We saw no sign naming the main street. An Art Institute and another colorful big sign appeared for Rosebud Sioux Indian Arts and Crafts, but they looked closed today. Sinte Gleska University had moved from the hill in Rosebud. Its entrance now in Mission displayed a huge bright sign in the Lakota colors of white, red, yellow, and black. Mission also now had its own traffic light and a Subway deli. The Antelope Motel had become the Antelope Country Inn, still with only a couple of cars in the lot. It was missing some dark siding with gaps in the gutters and cloudy windows, though the loiterers didn't seem to mind. We decided to stick with our only other lodging option at the Rosebud Casino's Quality Inn several miles outside of town.

But first, we took a detour down memory lane through Rosebud town. A Tribal Buffalo Project sign greeted us along the way. However, the buffalo must have roamed far from the road as we saw none this time. A weathering but upright metal sign now stood at the turn-off from Mission to Rosebud: "Welcome to the Land of the *Sicangu Lakota Oyate*—The Burnt Thigh Nation—Rosebud South Dakota."

The road to Rosebud surprised us by becoming a four-lane highway closer to the new hospital. I knew the population had doubled since we'd left, from 736 to now about 1500, but could there really be that much traffic out here? We gawked at the cluster of buildings: Tribal Land Enterprise, a Yoga and Meditation center, a church, more court buildings, a transportation center with school buses, day care center, a gas station with convenience store, and fairgrounds in the widened area. All new since our time there. One mobile home was covered with tires on the roof. We wondered whether they might be for added insulation or maybe to keep the roof from blowing off when those prairie winds kicked up. Many solitary mobile homes had tipis or frames in the yard, as well as a multitude of junked cars. We also saw some newer wooden housing tracts, looking sturdier and with bigger yards than the ones we remembered.

Continuing on, the main drag revealed the old "Pill Hill," now a surprisingly small bare patch of dirt where the old hospital had been torn down. We felt ghosts and heard echoes from the past as we found our early housing. The brick apartment building remained where Judy and I had watched the ER door so we could leave to avoid being called in. The different apartments for Rose, Steph, and me where we'd had the legendary fondue party were still occupied. We even think we found Beeson's old now-beat-up trailer by the end of the road. Continuing up the hill to the center of Rosebud, we found the Tribal Office, more older houses, and the two roads to either St. Francis or to Ghost Hawk Park and Crow Dog's Paradise. What we didn't find was the new hospital. It's not that big a place, so where was it?

We retraced our route back down to the widened area and found a turn-off which we'd missed earlier when gawking. This road led to a new water tower, WIC building (Women, Infants, and Children program), alcohol treatment center, Veterans Services, Community Resources, Dialysis Center, ambulance, and several other supportive services surrounding the large modern-looking turtle-shaped hospital. Built in 1989, it included a parking area for dozens of cars. I don't recall much of a parking lot at the old hospital, but not many folks had cars back then. We had been noticing a lot more cars and SUVs, and fewer rezmobiles. The public health nursing department had grown from the couple of nurses in a closet that we'd known to now filling an entire building. A Rehab building joined this cluster, now offering physical therapy. Solar panels dotted some of the buildings.

Having fully satisfied our curiosity for now, we made our way back through Mission and turned toward the Rosebud Casino, about 22 miles south at the border of the Rosebud Reservation and Nebraska. We saw the first Rosebud Casino sign a couple miles south of Mission, about 20 miles from the casino. We noticed far fewer casino signs here compared to the Pine Ridge Prairie Winds Casino, which was well-advertised in the Black Hills and on the approach. We passed lots of Black Angus cattle on tribal land, again a source of income whether the tribe owned the cattle or collected rent on the grazing land. More small settlements, with a few rezmobiles and plenty of junked cars for parts or shelter or whatever.

And then there it was, with a huge tall sign. The Rosebud Casino stands beside the Quality Inn and a gas station with convenience store, and nothing else for miles beyond the huge parking lot. Inside the modern motel lobby hangs a beautiful handmade quilt in a rosebud pattern surrounding the traditional morning star. The indoor pool we passed held cloudy green water. Signs posted in the lobby and hallways said, "No Alcohol." There was a one hundred dollar fine for drinking. "Smile the Camera is Watching You."

We saw three cars in the hotel parking lot, with about 2 dozen at the large casino. Our room was clean and quiet. In the hotel's information booklet, all the business ads were for Valentine, Nebraska, 9 miles south, whereas there were none at all for any Rosebud businesses. A giant wind turbine towered over the back lot, with a prominent sign in the hall about all the dozens of unlikely corporate partners: Dave Matthews Band, Indigo Girls, Green Mountain Coffee, Ben and Jerry's. With average prairie winds of fourteen mph, harnessing this power could make a real difference. After a couple of days with no turbine movement in the constant wind, we asked at the desk and were told that they were waiting for a part. I wondered for how long?

After spending a long day in the car, we opted for the prime rib buffet at the casino, hand-carved by an attendant in a chef's jacket. Sides included instant mashed or baked potatoes and salad bar with white lettuce, carrot sticks, and raw broccoli. Soft serve ice cream and assorted pies for dessert in the large cinderblock cafeteria-style room, hung with beautiful Lakota murals and artwork. This was certainly a lavish display for this area. All for a bargain $12.99 each. We ventured into the casino with our $5 hotel gambling voucher, but the assault of the flashing lights and bells from the video slot machines did not tempt us. Although we wanted to support the tribe, we were quickly overcome by the cigarette smoke. Steph saw a sign for a separate bar way at the back, and we headed the other way toward our room. The hallway connecting the casino to the hotel displayed a large portrait gallery of historic tribal Chiefs: Spotted Tail, Iron Shell, Hollow Horn Bear, and Two Strike.

We asked the young desk clerk whether the casino was making any money and how it was spent. He seemed taken aback by the question, but after a pause he replied that "Yes, it makes some money" and vaguely said that "the tribe spreads it around. Last year they helped with heating bills. The money doesn't get paid to individual tribal members." We later heard that there are too many tribal members for the casino to really help most people. "It doesn't give enough jobs. People without money go and lose, while the rich ranchers are the ones that win."

The sign by the desk indicated a change in the weather from today's sunny 90s to a cloudy high tomorrow in the 60s, but the night was still clear. We stepped out the back door to see the stars in the big sky, enjoying the fresh breeze. The security lights dimmed the stars even here but we appreciated the safety factor. We looked back gratefully on another wonderful day, amazed to be back in Rosebud after more than forty years.

Tomorrow we would visit the university and hospital. Would anyone really talk with us this time? Would we get the real story of what's been happening at the hospital? Would we find anybody we had known so long ago? I read my new book *The Lakota Way,* seeking strength and inspiration to prepare me until sleep would bring us to the new day.

Monday morning, 9/12/16, Rosebud—Sinte Gleska University.

A crimson and golden sunrise haloed the lone tree in the parking lot. I was awake at dawn with thoughts bouncing around in my head. I felt excited / anxious / nervous about approaching people to interview, and about whether anybody would agree to talk with me at all.

Having been greeted on this journey by a rainbow, a bison, and an eagle, my heart held cautious hope as we began our first full day in Rosebud. In 1973 trouble had roiled and boiled over, with so much anger turned inward and outward. But by 2016 two generations had had some time to process different experiences and perhaps also some healing...

We met a bulky talkative guy at the hotel breakfast from Sturgis, in western South Dakota. He worked for Veterans' housing assistance in Rosebud, Pine Ridge, and Standing Rock. He said the vets' housing waitlist is about 5 yrs. We'd seen signs of a large veterans' presence out here with Vet's Services, special vet areas at the casino, and sadly, a huge modern veterans' cemetery. I asked his thoughts on the pipeline situation. He'd not gone to the protest camp near Standing

Rock. He said the pipeline project is about 60% finished now, and it would likely go through. He implied his support for the pipeline. Odds are certainly in the pipeline's favor in this David and Goliath fight. (Locally, the pipeline was known as the black poisonous snake.) But I felt that the peaceful coming together of so many tribal nations and international support with so much positive energy certainly had inspired hope to many.

Steph and I decided to start our Rosebud queries at the Sinte Gleska University, thinking the Lakota Studies department could offer us some information. Pulling into the dirt drive and parking beyond the big colorful entrance sign, we saw another smaller signpost with slats pointing to various buildings: Earth Bldg., Voc. Ed., Lakota Studies, Day Care, Greenhouse. The Lakota Studies sign pointed rightward toward two unmarked buildings.

Deep Breath.

We shrugged and chose the log cabin over its nondescript neighbor. I knocked and opened the main door revealing a kitchenette, but no people.

My "Hello" was returned from a back room, followed promptly by a pleasant dark-haired woman. "How can I help you?" she asked with interest in her eyes.

Another deep breath. The words came slowly as I carefully processed my thoughts to explain my mission, which felt foreign even to me. After exchanging introductions, I explained that I was writing a book of the stories that we had collected while working in the hospital so long ago in 1973-4. I found myself returning to Rosebud after over forty years, now as a writer, to revisit the people and land of the younger nurse of my past. I offered the list of names which I would need permission to mention in the book.

The woman, Denise One Star, took the list and immediately jotted contacts for several families, noting that many "had passed." Not surprising since we'd been there over forty years ago, and several had been sick and elderly even back then. We knew some had passed on as we'd cared for them in their last hours, but now we were hoping for family contacts. Denise came to Lame Deer's name on the list and said we should talk to this medicine man's daughter, Maxine Bordeaux. She would have a lot of valuable information. We could find her in the university administration building at the Antelope Lake

Campus. "It's near the big tipi for Lakota Studies, down the road, over there," she said, pointing vaguely.

It turns out that Denise One Star was not in Lakota Studies as we had thought, but she worked in Allied Health as a life coach. Unaware that the one-building community college I had known had grown to two university campuses, we were in the wrong area entirely. We'd been misled by signs that did not match reality, a recurring theme. But Denise was so kind, and I certainly needed some coaching for my first book project. Before we left, Denise mentioned that her grant was running out, and that it was hard to get teachers for the LPN (Licensed Practical Nurse), EMT (Emergency Medical Technician), and CNA (Certified Nurse Aide) programs. Staff turnover throughout the university is a problem, especially in the administration, she said

This visit—a surreal backdrop of vaguely familiar territory—was proving to be a sharp contrast from our first time in Rosebud.

Returning to the car, we asked each other if Denise meant the dirt road behind the buildings near the little pond – was that Antelope Lake? Or did she mean for us to get back onto Highway 18, which is what we did. The local map we'd proudly remembered to bring was 42 years old, and some things had changed. Out here the GPS signal was sketchy and unreliable. We drove past a sign for the tribal buffalo herd without seeing any buffalo, and continued all the way to Okreek, 15 miles east. We knew that was too far. We turned back and found the sign for the Antelope Campus and the tall tipi only a couple of miles from the main campus, but all this was hidden by a hill and trees from our original direction. Only a 30-mile detour.

Prairie dogs greeted us at the log cabin administration building, the closest we'd been to the creatures yet. Through the deserted foyer and into an office, we told the first person we saw that were looking for Maxine Bordeaux.

"You found her. How can I help you?" A substantial woman with a neutral expression sat behind a cluttered desk, appearing to be juggling several tasks.

Deep breath again.

I introduced us with the same general spiel and showed her the list of names when she asked. She pointed out the photos of her dad, Lame Deer behind her desk. She added contacts for several families, and when I asked about hiring a student to help me find the families, Maxine generously offered to help me approach the families. Even better, she suggested that when I return with a publisher's proper permission forms that I should give a presentation for the families, with readings from the book, and many families would come to meet me. Brilliant! I had already decided that I needed to be the one to talk to the families, in case they had questions, plus I wanted to meet these people and hear their stories. Maxine validated my plan saying, "Yes, they need to look into your eyes and see your heart." We talked about what gifts I could offer at the presentation—coffee, tobacco, sage or cedar smudge sticks, and I may knit some scarves. More ideas were coming as this phase of the project unfolded.

Although we didn't have much chance to talk that day, Maxine has become an invaluable resource, and our friendship has bloomed as we worked together on this book and a few side projects. She later told me that as a girl she had gathered medicinal plants for Lame Deer to use in his healing ceremonies, and she had met many people as they came to her father for help. She was the only Indian to graduate in her 1969 high school class in Winner. She said the others dropped out mainly because of the intense racist bullying. After graduation Maxine attended two universities, but each time she had to return to Rosebud to care for family members. She took part in the relocation and assimilation program, moving to California with the goal of learning a trade. However, as with many others in these programs, the pressures of the experience led to a troubled time in her life. Later when she met her husband Ramero, he helped her to find her spiritual roots, untangle the knots of her life and return to Rosebud to stay. Maxine and Ramero had three children, but sadly, only one daughter now survives, along with a large treasured extended family.

Back at the university, Maxine returned to my list of names, also remarking on several folks who had passed on. When she saw the name of Lorna Her Many Horses, our beloved colleague, she said with a smile, "She's crazy." Stopping at Ben Black Bear's name, she said that his daughter Sandra teaches in Lakota Studies and we really should talk to her. We could find her across the parking lot in the tall tipi building. Bingo! We thanked Maxine heartily, and hustled into the tipi school.

The light and airy atmosphere of the semicircular room surprised me, with a skylight and many windows looking out onto the small rippling Antelope Lake. We approached the vacant reception desk, and a woman with a friendly smile and sparkling dark eyes appeared from the office in back. I offered my intro, and I asked for Sandra Black Bear. The receptionist, Gina One Star, who is related to Denise One Star, told us that Sandra had a class at 1 p.m. but she could call her to see if she'd come earlier to talk with us. It was noon, as we looked at the many posters decorating the high slanting walls: local and regional cultural activities, meetings to Help Our Children, and SGU's 45th anniversary celebration in 2015. Gina returned and yes, Sandra would come in early for us.

Meanwhile, Gina offered us coffee. She also had a huge pot of soup on the stove she was making for staff and students. "I loaded it with vegetables and waved a little meat over it," she smiled. This mother hen also had zucchini bread on the table and was putting a birthday cake in the oven. Gina sat to chat with us while we waited for Sandra. What a great time we had getting to know her. She had gone to one of those legendary boarding schools, which she glossed over. Gina had studied art in college in Santa Fe, then moved to Minnesota, where she got involved in AIM. She travelled with the inner circles there, as far as Hawaii, and showed me Clyde Bellecourt's weathered AIM business card with his still current contact info. She showed us the beautiful eagle painting she'd done for the cover of a publication by the U.S. Geological Survey, and she had given a talk on eagles to that group in Washington, DC. I mentioned my impression of Lakota people's increasing interest in the old traditions. She agreed that generally many of the youth were more grounded and stable now, one or two generations after the boarding school experiences.

A student asked Gina about the bus schedule, so then I asked her about local transportation now. Gina told us that "a millionaire back East" had donated money for SGU buses. As we talked, the aromas of the soup and cake filled the area and warmed the cool cloudy day. She said she loved the water, and I was glad she had a view of the lake. Then Gina was off to a meeting.

About 10 minutes before her class, Sandra breezed in, saying she'd been held up in traffic. Hard to imagine at this hour in the open land. I asked where she'd come from, and she mentioned several small communities that I couldn't quite place. I was thinking maybe they did need that four-lane road in Rosebud. As she plunked her tote bag down, she said. "Something smells good" and in a single motion went for a hunk of the zucchini bread on the table. Sandra was about our age too, with flawless mocha skin and a set of creases under the outer corners of her eyes in just the right places. She spoke of her parents in St. Francis teaching traditional Lakota crafts and music wherever they could find a space. They were passionate about passing on their culture in a time when it was forbidden to practice those traditions. Unlike Gina, Sandra offered little eye contact. In retrospect, I felt a little as though we were being measured up. Would I be worth her time and energy? Could I be trusted with information? After Sandra had gone to her class, Steph and I decided that the remark about traffic had to be a joke and we should have laughed. Sandra was so deadpan. I hoped we could work together. I liked her. She did give me her personal cell number, perhaps a deposit on a relationship.

MONDAY AFTERNOON, 9/12/16, ROSEBUD HOSPITAL & MORE.

After our full morning at SGU we needed a lunch break to regroup and assess our progress. Subway offered some warm soup and colorful vegetables, scarce for travelers to find around here.

Fortified with lunch, we headed to the newer turtle-shaped hospital with the prayer shawl and baby blanket we had each knitted for the occasion. The covered main entrance led to a large reception area. We asked at the front desk for the Director of Nurses, hoping someone would be available to show us around. We were directed down a hall toward the left. As we entered the administration area we saw two women, aged about 30 years apart. The younger one asked how she could help us. I launched into my spiel, now smoother with practice. When I said that we'd worked at the hospital in 1973 she interrupted. With a grand wave of her arm toward the other woman, she said,

"This the woman you need to speak with, Yvonne Reynolds."

My eyes bugged out. "Vonnie?" I gasped.

"I remember you," she replied with a grin. "I'm still here after 44 years, still working for the DON." She had also been our unit clerk, doing double duty. Her long dark wavy hair was now a trendy smooth bob to her ears, and silver like ours. We presented our knitted offerings and asked if she could find a home for them. She held up the baby blanket, saying,

"I'm keeping this one for myself. I just had a new grandbaby. My daughter is a nurse upstairs and will give this other one a good home. We just had a lady who didn't have anything, but she left. There'll be another."

We swapped some old hospital stories and remembered lots of the same people. When I mentioned Lorna Her Many Horses, she said, "She's so crazy" with a grin, like everyone else had this morning. Vonnie sent greetings to Dr. Tosi who had been her doctor. She'd liked Mr. Arnold, who'd become a DON too. "It was like family back then," she said. "You could come back to work here now. We need the help," she smiled. That led me to ask about the Emergency Room situation. As we spoke, a man arrived in a black polo shirt reporting for duty and asking where to go. He was flatly pointed in the right direction. Vonnie appeared uncomfortable talking about the ER even in low voices here in the public reception area. She was becoming anxious and agitated so I pressed no further, though my curiosity consumed me. We hugged, and I was so grateful for that amazing connection. We came away without a tour of the hospital, but we'd gotten so much more.

We stopped at the nearby alcohol treatment center, as I wanted to get a sense of how things were these days. As we waited with the receptionist in the quiet foyer, I studied a poster of a woman standing proudly in native dress by a badlands scene. The caption read, "To survive, we must begin to know sacredness. The pace which most of us live prevents this." Eventually a brusque woman appeared, the director. When I explained my goal, she said she was too busy to talk with us, but when asked she reluctantly gave an email contact. Then she offered another colleague's email, saying, "He likes to talk."

Next stop was the tribal office, up the hill. We entered into a medium-sized room. Several people looked up from their desks. I started my intro, attempting eye contact with a few. One woman about our age responded. Her name plate read Cynthia Crow Eagle. At first, she referred us to the Community Health Resources offices in the blue trailer back down the road, but then relented and looked at my list of names. She commented on those who had passed, and she added a few more contacts. I asked how to know which family member to approach for permission, and she said, "they'll tell you." Oh. It was that simple. At one point, Cynthia was straining so hard to remember a long-lost nurse's son that she actually pounded her head with her fist. I gently told her that she could copy my list and contact me later. She said, "You won't go away empty-handed, because you've made a friend." Bless her. She did email me later with more contacts, again telling me she's my friend.

Our heads and hearts were full from the day's interviews. We took the road out to St. Francis, down another memory lane. The Indian Museum we remembered with the Ghost Dance shirts disappointed us with a sign stating that it was closed from Labor Day to Memorial Day. It looked unloved, with torn screens and a rusty door. The St. Francis Indian School contrasted with its modern buildings, buses, playground, and large playing fields. On the same large church campus, we found a modern Recovery Center, new Mission building, two old boarded up buildings where I'd gone to pow wows, and a sizable lavender stucco church. The sign named St. Charles of Borromeo, someone I'd learned of in northern Italy. I'd also seen his statue in France. His infamous nose was portrayed smaller here; maybe not as famous a nose here as in Europe. He got around. I wondered about the connection with this area, if any. We also saw the statue of Kateri Tekakwitha, recently sainted, who is from Judy's part of upstate New York. I love when the cosmos offers us threads of connection. We didn't see or hear a human soul as we wandered around. Just a bird singing in the small glade of trees as the boughs bent in the gentle everlasting breeze.

Heading back to Valentine for dinner, route 20E in Nebraska was strikingly better than the same-sized route 18 through Indian Country in South Dakota. We didn't think it was the NE-SD state distinction, as Hwy 18 also seemed to have different standards inside and outside the rez. We saw just one sign for Rosebud Casino east of Valentine. That makes a total of two.

In Valentine we found our old grocery store, and eventually found the main street with the hardware store where we'd bought the Thanksgiving paper goods, the Christmas ornaments and the fondue pots. The Western wear shop was still there where I'd bought Rick's cowboy hat, but it was closed by the time we found it. McDonald's had now made the scene—we would have loved that, back in the day. Subway and Pizza Hut had replaced the truck stops here too. We did find the small Bunkhouse Café, where we ordered the chicken fried steak we'd thought we'd be eating all week. It came with white gravy, instant or baked potato with white oleo or sour cream, white iceberg lettuce and ranch dressing. Even as a Swede, I don't think I've ever had a completely white meal before. The other vegetable option was onion rings. We felt vegetable deprived, and we thought of Gina's aromatic rich vegetable soup and zucchini bread.

The only waitress in the nearly empty café was our age, petite, with a pinched face that never cracked a smile. We hoped she would feel better soon, whether physically, emotionally, or both. For dessert we ordered fry bread to go—another white food. We didn't know where else we could find this Lakota treat while here.

After such a heavy meal, we looked for a place to walk, other than doing laps around the casino parking lot. We remembered that Fort Niobrara was nearby, but it somehow eluded us. We did find a "Cowboy Trail," which rewarded us with golden vistas as we walked briskly in the fresh wind for an hour before dusk. The elevated footbridge across the Niobrara River connected the ridges of the valley and gave us a dizzying thrill.

Back at the hotel, we now felt we'd earned our fry bread. We opened our Styrofoam box to find several little lumps of fried dough with honey. They were heavy and not the light flat rounds we'd remembered at the pow wows—these seemed more like Mexican sopaipillas. It didn't help that they were cold by now. While munching, we called Rose in Wyoming, to report in on our trip so far. She felt united with us in spirit and said she wants to come next time we're in Rosebud. We told her of our days here so far. The no alcohol /no smoking signs reminded her of a group of men who'd volunteered to come and sit with people in DTs when she was working at the hospital. I don't remember this. We knew of no AA, and with hardly any phones we're not sure how the volunteers got the message to come. Moccasin telegraph, perhaps?

What we didn't see this time was drunken people stumbling in the streets.

What we did see was some resurgence of traditional values and education.

I decided to call my new contact, Lorna's daughter, Kathi Her Many Horses. She gave me Lorna's cell number, saying that if Lorna wanted to meet with us tomorrow she would take her wherever she wanted to go. Lorna didn't take long to remember us and agreed to meet, saying, "I'll be the one with gray hair and the shape." Us too, I guess. We couldn't wait to see her, after all these years. Unbelievable.

Stephanie started our day by making double-strength coffee in our room—Hallelujah! Finally, coffee here we could taste. I'm definitely bringing my own coffee when I return though. And I agree with Maxine that it would make great gifts for the families when I do the presentation. Steph and I had the breakfast room to ourselves today, with just the TV yammering the morning news. I was a little disappointed not to be able to glean any more local information from other breakfast guests, but this dismay would evaporate as the day progressed.

Driving back up to Mission, we reflected on the different vibe here on the rez now. I felt some spiritual resurgence in the people we've met. The poverty and problems are still here, but we felt overall less poverty of spirit than when we'd lived here. Of course, this visit was very brief and in an entirely different context. In 1973 we saw so much anger, turned both inward and outward. We also noted that so many of the family contacts on our list were employed, though unemployment remains high, at about 70 percent. I believe these contacts were selected for us because many were the most educated family members.

Coming back north from the casino, we saw now that the sign for the Soldier Woman Art & Gift Gallery in Mission had an arrow pointing to a house set back from the road. We pulled into the gravel drive to a cute garden by the house, but the shop was closed.

A man came out, saying, "It's 9:45 and we open at 10, so I might as well open now for you."

He unlocked the door to another world, and my heart sang. Beautiful handmade beaded moccasins filled two display cases, in sizes from newborn to huge. Fringed and embroidered dancing shawls hung on a small rack with jingle dresses, near the feather bustles and headgear for pow wows. A wall of jewelry and accessories, some made with dyed porcupine quills, some finely beaded, some silver and turquoise in the Southwest style. Purses, bags, jackets, quilts and all kinds of treasure filled this beautiful shop. A large glass case of handmade wooden flutes stood in the center, but alas, none local and none in Richard Fool Bull's distinctive painted style that I had bought from him. He was right. He was the last. But maybe someone would take up his art again someday, as interest in tradition resurges. We loaded up on gifts, and we took cards with the website info. I was thinking that this business card should be in the casino Quality Inn book among the ads from Valentine. Maybe a sampling could be sold at the casino too, where more folks might see it.

I called Lorna. She was waiting at the Turtle Creek grocery and café with her daughter, Kathi. I said we'd be right there, and we dashed off to the café on the hill. The grocery used to be a tribal co-op but was now privately owned. It had been just another empty hillside back in our day.

We hustled through the grocery's impressive array of fresh produce, and into the clean modest café on the right. Pausing at the entrance, we scanned the room for Lorna, as everyone looked up at the only non-natives there. Spotting them in a booth by the window, we breezed across the room to exchange hugs and get re-acquainted. Now with permed white hair, her petite face had weathered into a lovely collection of lines, somehow echoing the landscape's texture. Lorna introduced Marshall, "the man I boss around now," saying her husband Leo had died several years ago. Marshall excused himself from the ladies, but Kathi stayed to chat with us. She was the youngest, adopted to the family and Lorna said, "Best thing I ever did."

We spoke of folks we'd known, and Lorna caught us up on several names I'd forgotten after 40+ years. They looked at my list of names, and Lorna told me that Thomas Wolf Guts had been a code talker in WWII, but I've yet to find anyone with family contact info for him. Ray was the name of the guy I'd been trying to remember who'd caught the rattlesnakes on the hill. He died. Kathi mentioned her godfather "Uncle Leonard," referring to Leonard Crow Dog. I remarked how intimidating he had been to us, and she said that he's in a wheelchair now, living in Valentine. He'd held a sun dance last weekend though, back at Crow Dog's Paradise. Kathi mentioned someone she is very close to, "a *hunka* sister," spiritually adopted family. I said that Steph is my *hunka* sister, and Lorna said with a smile, "After all this time, I guess she is." She remembered all the Rosebuddies in the book, and she asked for names of a few of the other nurses: Bev Wickham, Lynn Romanowski. She said to say Hi to Dr. Tosi—"He was my doctor and I really liked him."

We recalled delivering that baby together, and she said she delivered one herself after that. It was a friend of hers in the hospital, and nobody came to help them. Afterwards she said to her friend, "Please turn over." Lorna gave her a slap on the backside, saying, "Don't you get pregnant again if it means I ever have to deliver another baby!"

Lorna told us more of her family—her son Randy had married Lucy Reifel and they had kids. The marriage broke up a while ago, and he died of a heart attack this past spring. It's been very hard for Lorna. Son Chico is still dancing and winning prizes. Son Emil is still a curator at the Smithsonian Museum of the American Indian, and she shared his business card. Lorna commented," I never wanted to work. I just wanted to stay home and take care of my family. So, I quit a while back, as soon as I could. Did I tell I went to nursing school? I didn't like it so I never finished." Her eyes carry a deep sadness from her recent loss, and she has a persistent cough, increasing as she got tired.

"You'll have to come back in the summer. We'll have a picnic so you can meet the whole family. We can go to my son's place in Montana. You'd like it there."

Kathi left for an appointment, and we updated Lorna on our own families and lives. I reminded her of some more of the incidents we'd shared at the old hospital, and she said, "I want to read that book."

Lorna wouldn't talk much about Rosebud's current hospital situation, but she won't use their services. When I asked her about it, she dismissed us silently with a long dark look. She went to Rapid City for back surgery, "and they dropped me. The doctor told me I should sue them, and I sure could use the money, but I won't do that."

She spoke of local gang activity, involved with meth, and warned us to stay away from the new bar. She's still our mother hen, bless her. We reassured her that we're back in our hotel room by 8 or 9. She said she's been to the casino, and she asked if the hotel was clean. Said that a dryer sheet can keep the bugs away. Good to know.

After three wonderful hours, Lorna was starting to get restless with back discomfort and her cough was nagging. She tried to call Marshall a few times, having trouble seeing and navigating her flip phone. I offered to help, but she declined. We offered to take her home, but no. Marshall eventually got the message and came to pick her up. She pushed herself slowly up from the table, wincing occasionally, and we each took an arm to walk her outside to the truck. I hope we didn't tire her out too much. We exchanged long hugs. I told her I'd make her a prayer shawl and when she puts it on she should feel the hug.

She has it now, in her chosen colors of red and blue, with touches of Lakota black, white and yellow along with the red.

By then, the Turtle Creek Café had closed their limited grill, so Steph and I headed back to the Subway for more veggies in our lunch, to digest our wonderful morning and plan our next move. I reflected how I was enjoying the tempo and the nuances of the local speech. Some words sounded clipped and swallowed, others drawn out with a hint of a musical lilt. The use of the expression "I'n'it" for "isn't it." It's difficult for me to describe, but it brought me back to our days at the hospital, in a good way.

Kathi texted me later: "It was a good morning. I didn't want to leave. Mom was so happy. I like seeing her happy. Thank you for the visit!" Kathi and I are Facebook friends now and Lorna's getting a sneak peek at the book in her own personal large print copy.

DAKOTAS JOURNAL, TUESDAY EVENING, 9/13, JODY
AND FINAL TOUR.

The afternoon began with a stop at the light blue trailer for Community Health Services with the dual goals of finding more family contacts plus identifying resources that book readers could support. Two roaming dogs greeted us by leaning in for hugs and wagging enthusiastic tails. They didn't seem as skinny as those we remembered. The main door opened to a reception area with two women, again about 30 years apart in age. I did my intro, and the younger woman behind the desk said we should talk with the other one, Jody, who had been there far longer. She was on our contact list as our ambulance driver's daughter. Following in the family footsteps, she was a driver for Community Health, using her own car to transport clients to appointments. They'd call ahead and book a ride—for a fee. CHS does give some free (subsidized) rides, mostly for drug and alcohol addiction services, she says. Encouraged, I commented that there seem to be more resources for this now. Does she think things are getting better? No, because her passengers are getting court-ordered treatment, they aren't motivated, and they relapse into a downward spiral. Also, meth and prescription drugs are now a big problem. "The hospital can't treat them, so they give pain meds." I didn't get a chance to clarify whether she meant that the hospital can't treat the source of pain or the addiction.

Unlike many we'd attempted to ask, Jody seemed quite comfortable sharing her opinion about the hospital issues as I sat beside her in the open room. Words flowed in an emphatic torrent from this petite dynamo with blazing brown eyes and short-cropped salt-and-pepper hair.

"Health care is going downhill. It's going backward, worse than when you were here. It's just a Band-Aid station now. Prisoners get better care than we get. There was a doc that was fired from the Indian Health Service, but he was hired by the contractors, so he's still in the ER. Even though the ER is back open with the contract doctors, they still ship everyone out to Martin, Winner, or Valentine. They don't know how to take care of people. If you have a broken finger, they don't know how to set it so they even send you out for that. They get vital signs and wait for a plane or ambulance. Ambulances have paramedics now, but the distance is a killer. We've lost a bunch of people."

"I hurt my back and they flew me to Rapid City to see a doc there. I got a bill for $54,000. I can't pay that. The tribe can't pay that. And we shouldn't. Where's the free health care that's in the treaty? IHS (Indian Health Service) is way in the hole and they just keep borrowing into the future, using next year's budget so now that will run out sooner.

"IHS is supposed to reimburse the contractor for my airlift from here, but they're so slow and delay the payment, so my credit is ruined. Legal services won't help. They have to practice law for those on the bottom of the totem pole.

"We all have insurance now since Obamacare. But we have to pay for insurance. I can't afford it. The tribe can't afford it. The treaty says we shouldn't have to pay. It's hocus pocus."

The Affordable Care Act laws mandate that the tribe as an employer pay $4.5 million per year in health insurance or $2.5 million in fines, despite the fact that in exchange for land the tribe was promised free health care.

She spoke of her son who came to the Rosebud ER and was diagnosed with two broken ribs. He was discharged and told to see a trauma specialist. Jody was instructed that she could drive him the three hours to Sioux Falls the next day.

"He was in so much pain I took him right away in my car. In Sioux Falls they found a torn bleeding lung, a broken back, more broken

148

ribs, and told me I never should have driven him myself. He could have died. They sent him to a medical center in Denver. He was in surgery for nine and a half hours and came out with a steel plate in his chest. He's still recovering. And they (Rosebud) said it was just 2 broken ribs. They can't even read an X-ray."

Jody said they used to have some good docs. Together we recalled some that I'd worked with. I'd also read about another, who had stayed for several years and was widely loved.

"Emil Redfish was a good Physician's Assistant too. He was South Dakota's PA of the year, but he left and lives in Arlington now. Lorenzo Stars was a local doc, but he moved to Sanford. It's so bad here the good ones don't want to stay any more.

"The administration is top-heavy, and people are just riding their time out. They don't care. We have 5 community health nurses making good salaries, but they don't do many visits. Same with the alcohol and drug treatment center. Folks there too are just waiting to retire."

"But we're also at fault. The drunks' fake seizures, taking up space and time at the hospital. They used to just go to jail, but now it's called an illness, so they go for court-ordered treatment. Some people in rehab are from off the rez, taking up our beds."

I asked about Alcoholics Anonymous meetings and Jody said there is one in St. Francis. I had thought there were more. I had read about some sober pow wows with no alcohol allowed, but she shot down that concept. I brought up the historic growing gathering at the DAPL pipeline site, and how it seemed to be energizing some people with hope. I asked about the renewed interest in the old Lakota traditions and she said,

"It's half and half. Some are looking for a quick fix. In the 70s, AIM, with their alcohol, violence and drugs—now died and forgotten. Until we stop blaming our past, and the government, how can we stand up? We have to find our own strength.

"We don't want payment for the Black Hills. We've always refused payment. It's still our land. But other people live there now. I don't think we'll ever get it back. We need to work on problems closer to home that affect our daily lives: health care, drugs, alcohol, and transportation."

Before we left, I did ask about community resources that readers might be able to support. Jody hesitated, as Lorna had. She said, "Stick with non-natives with good intentions, like Habitat for Humanity, St. Francis Mission, Sicangu Child and Family Mission, Tree of Life Church." I got the impression that local projects tend to be more transient or intermittent, due to funding, effectiveness, or resource issues.

After a couple of intense hours, Jody ended our talk with," I have to go now and pick up my granddaughter, which is more important than talking to you, or anything else."

Wowza. No more interviews today. My brain was fried. We opted to drive past the crest of Rosebud center, and to look for Crow Dog's Paradise and the lakes down the hill with our old sketchy map.

As we digested some of Jody's words, we speculated that maybe the contract ER docs were from big hospitals where specialists are readily available. There, it is usual practice to stabilize and refer patients. Not a good fit for Rosebud where they need general practitioners and family docs for immediate help on site. And Rosebud definitely needs physicians of better quality than those Jody had described.

We drove past Ghost Hawk Park to find Crow Dog's Paradise. Since we knew he no longer lived there, this time we dared to slow down. We saw the frame of the sweat lodge conveniently placed near the Little White River for a water source to make steam and to douse the fire at the proper time. The bridge's official sign had now been changed to read: Little White River Crow Dog Bridge. A painted tire sign proclaimed Crow Dog's Paradise, as before. We looked at the hand-painted Security Booth of weathered boards with a Native logo, another tire Entrance sign, and a bower with a blue tarp on top of the pine boughs. Four dogs came running down the dirt drive, barking aggressively. The current security team, I presume.

Crow Dog's Paradise appeared to be well guarded even in his absence. I somehow got the feeling that he knew we were there, even from his home in Valentine. I could feel his presence, and I did not feel welcome even now. Just past here, the road was closed to Bead's and Chases Women Lakes. We tried to see if local traffic could get through, but no, the road was completely closed. We tried the smaller road up the hill behind Crow Dog's but it dead-ended in a small neighborhood where we again felt intrusive.

We turned back to drive through Ghost Hawk Park, meeting a family of fuzzy wild turkey chicks at the roadside. The park had a deserted vibe, with only one middle-aged guy sitting on a picnic table by a camper. It felt less than safe. Some wisps of memories teased us but refused to form completely.

We headed back through Rosebud to say goodbye, and we decided to continue eastward to Winner in hopes of a nice last dinner. The extra 90 miles round trip might be worth it, as we'd exhausted the options in Rosebud, Mission, and Valentine. Besides, Winner had been part of our old stomping grounds where we'd gotten some groceries and bought my car Shigella. We passed the tribal buffalo land again, but this time they were out on the hill for our send-off. Lots of horses grazed in the hills too, with manes blowing in the ever-present prairie wind. Bright sunflower fields with beautiful vibrant blooms glowed in the waning golden sunshine of the big sky. We passed through the tiny community of Okreek where we'd turned around just yesterday looking for Maxine, Sandra and Lakota Studies at SGU. Deer grazed in the distance, and this time they weren't hay rolls, as some of the "antelope" we'd seen previously.

Finally, we reached Winner, hungry and tired. We drove past Main Street off Hwy 18, finding only a McDs, Pizza Hut, and China Buffet. We would have loved it in the 70s, but now it was not what we had in mind. Backtracking to cruise Main Street, we found closed and neglected buildings, two sketchy bars and no cafes. So, we checked the road atlas and headed south to Ainsworth, Nebraska, munching on our emergency snack of nuts. We passed the town of Colome, reminding me of Ron Colombe in South Carolina who was the inspiration for this book's title, *Magic and Tragic*, and who'd said to me, "If enough people read it maybe it can make a difference."

I'm working on it, Ron. You started me on this expanded path.

A small herd of six-point deer greeted us right by the roadside, gilded by the setting sun. The sight drew us in to stop for a photo as they posed so beautifully in the grass. Our ninety- mile dinner detour had been ambitious, but now we'd be close to making a two hundred mile square before we got back to Rosebud's casino. Next time my dining expectations here will be tamed. Although we felt hungry and tired, Stephanie and I were enjoying our extended good-bye tour.

We finally got to Ainsworth at 7:30, finding only the ubiquitous Subway and Pizza Hut, which also had been in Valentine and Winner. It was time to eat anyway. We did manage to find a few veggies at the salad bar and ordered some more on the pizza, by now feeling very grateful for any food. The décor surprised us, consisting of pastel stuffed bunnies all around the ceiling rail, and a running shoe stuck to the ceiling holding another stuffed bunny. The place was nearly full of families and youths in team uniforms enjoying their evening out.

Fifty more miles in the darkening twilight to complete our detour square back to "home" at the casino. The three-quarter moon and bright stars kept us company, along with some country tunes fading in and out on the radio.

We reviewed another full day of miracles as we gratefully tumbled into our beds. We were deeply moved by the warm welcomes we'd encountered this time. We'd found old friends to visit and met new ones. Plus, we'd discovered many echoes from the past. We'd found many more resources and signs of hope in the community, but we'd also encountered a lot of the same problems, some worse. Tomorrow we head out, too soon.

DAKOTAS JOURNAL, WEDNESDAY, 9/13 HOMEWARD.

We made a quick detour to the SGU bookstore for my last-minute purchase of a book about the 1973 Wounded Knee events, and Steph bought some herbs for her Master Gardener friends. We spoke with the cashier, Crystal, because yesterday in the shop we'd overheard her talking with a colleague about better marketing for Rosebud's businesses. They'd said they thought more efforts could be made at the casino, such as a gift shop. We agreed with that and also suggested more local Rosebud advertising such as for the Soldier Woman gift shop and the SGU bookstore in the back of the hotel booklet, to join the Valentine businesses. Maybe more advertising for the casino itself? Crystal thanked us politely and said she'd still be at the bookstore when I come back, hopefully next summer. We found it encouraging to see interest in promoting local businesses.

Turning north toward White River we passed a large cemetery for Sioux veterans, marked by a tall tipi sculpture at the gate. Lorna had told us that most of these vets had been in the Viet Nam and Gulf Wars, many with PTSD. Native Americans are historically one of the largest groups in the military according to Sprague in his book, *Rosebud Sioux*. He reports that as high as fifty percent of American Indians are veterans. Lorna said that "a few kids enlist these days, for the opportunity to work."

Herds of horses grazing in the hills brought to mind our first glimpses of the rez in 1973. We'd each driven this road from the

Murdo exit on I-90 heading south back then, as we'd spotted the falling-down sign for the Rosebud Rez boundary amid the vast open prairie.

We wondered about Subway and Pizza Hut pushing out the all the old truck stop cafes and diners with chicken fried steak and homemade pie. On this trip we hadn't seen any drug stores – no chain CVS or Rite Aid nor any independent ones either. Not many other stores nor even a Walmart. Rosebud folks would use the hospital pharmacy for prescriptions, and the Dollar Store in Valentine or Mission for non-prescription items.

We passed some small communities, many with junked cars in the yard—"giving back to the land" as they said in the book *Neither Wolf nor Dog*—or maybe just using parts for repairs. Or perhaps they're just sitting there, dying in their tracks because owners have no money to fix or tow them. When no longer running and beyond repair they may be recycled for use as shelter or dog houses. We used to have patients living in junked cars who came to the hospital with gangrene feet in the minus-40-degree winters. The housing waitlist remains long out here.

Our Pandora oldie tunes continued to alternate with the Native flutes as the prairie scenery rolled by.

As soon as we hit I-90 in Murdo, the billboards assaulted us for Wall Drug and other tacky attractions. Interstates here mark the land of kitsch, perhaps to break up the monotony. Besides the world's largest cow sculpture in North Dakota, now we had the 1880s Town with a huge 25-foot prairie dog statue. Longhorn cattle grazed between the billboards, as we whizzed west on the open road. We passed the Buffalo Gap National Grassland again, this time on the northern edge. We noticed lots of derelict and boarded up buildings this week. Things don't tend to get razed and removed with all this open land, except for the old PHS Rosebud hospital.

We'd saved enough time to swing through the South Dakota section of Badlands National Park. This time we saw the Ben Reifel visitor center, named for Lucy Reifel's uncle, the senator. His name had been added to the sign sometime in the past 40 years. The land formations here are even more striking and dramatic than those in North Dakota. I finally saw my first bighorn sheep and more prairie dogs. Magnificent views, colorful cathedral spires and stark alien landscapes like the moon, somehow supported lifeforms of sage and yellow wildflowers with an intoxicating smell like Herbal Essence shampoo. This land of fossils feels ancient but keeps changing, actually moving northward an inch per year as the wind erodes and re-deposits sections. Occasional tumbleweeds blew across our path. We even saw a good-bye bison as we left the park.

At Wall Drug, we pulled in for a quick snack of their famous free ice water, 5-cent coffee and homemade pie. Of the several dining rooms to choose, we found ourselves sitting by a statue of Spotted Tail, Sinte Gleska. The coffee may have been famous, but still very weak by our standards.

WOW. What a journey. My heart was full. In just two days I'd gotten contacts for 90-percent of the people on my list, plus a whole team of advisors for finding and approaching more people, as well as adding historical and cultural details. I'd rekindled old friendships and started building new ones if all goes well. Stephanie and I tried to fathom why this trip was so different from our earlier time there. We felt respected as elders ourselves with our silver hair, and had been directed to talk with other elders, our peers. We each now have a different life experience. Two more generations have passed to offer perspective and more time for healing. I did feel that the Pipeline gathering was a positive influence giving people more hope and purpose. Plus, this time we were reaching out to healthier parts of the community rather than just remaining isolated in the hospital with our overwhelming jobs. And maybe it was just that our presence and interest demonstrated some level of caring to these people who have lost so much, yet still have much to share.

My next return won't take so long, and I'm looking forward to strengthening budding friendships, meeting families mentioned in the book, and making more contacts to help partner with some projects.

The last song we heard before returning the rental car at the Rapid City airport was *Feeling Groovy*. Indeed.

27. A: North Dakota sky. B: SGU sign confuses us. C: Approached by a bison.

28. D: Wounded Knee cemetery. E: Rosebud Reservation. F: Rosebud Town sign.
G: Lakota Studies tipi. H. Tribal office entrance.

29. I: Sinte Gleska University entrance. J: Steph delivers shawl to hospital. K: Regina One Star holds cover art she did for the U.S. Geological Survey publication.

30. L: Hand beaded moccasins for sale at Soldier Woman Gallery. M: Vonnie Reynolds with the baby blanket.

31. N: Badlands National Park. O: Crow Dog Bridge.

32. P: Badlands, Journey to Wounded Knee. Q: Judy, Stephen Tosi, Nancy and
Stephanie at the Red Lion Inn, 2015.

The Future – Act Locally

16. Mosquitos and bees: finding strength

"If you think you're too small to make a difference try sleeping with a mosquito in the same room." Dalai Lama

All of history has been marked with both days of darkness and days of promise. Recently, people seem to be waking up and mobilizing again, with a global restlessness. We do have the power to reinvent ourselves.

Several friends and family members who have read these stories of Rosebud have asked how they could help. In response, I have added this section as a starting point. The answers can be tricky, as true healing must and will come from within, rather than from the well-meaning efforts of an outsider. But everybody needs help sometimes, and surely more can be accomplished by putting our efforts together.

Working within established frameworks and existing programs has proven over time to be an efficient use of resources. However, many local projects in Rosebud may be intermittent, depending on available funding and resources. Local contacts must be verified and updated before sending any type of donation, but a few of the more established resources are included here. Some larger organizations have offered a longstanding source of support to the community, both local and farther-reaching. I don't pretend to have answers to fix all the complex challenges in Rosebud. But small efforts can add up to significant change. Many suggestions can be applied both to Rosebud, and more generally to other communities as well. I drew heavily from ideas in two books, *Hope in the Dark* by R. Solnit and *A Path Appears* by N. Kristoff and S. WuDunn. Another book by Joseph Marshall, *The Lakota Way,* was used to frame concepts in terms of traditional values, as it was in earlier chapters.

TRUTH. *Wowicake.* That which is real, the way the world is.
"Making an injury visible and public is often the first step in remedying it...What was long tolerated becomes intolerable; what was overlooked becomes obvious." Solnit writes in *Hope in the Dark.* While *Magic and Tragic Rosebud* has touched briefly on the path of Native American history, many people remain unaware of these truths which have been buried in a whitewashed view of history. Native

Americans continue to dig for their own lost stories. Sharing some of the history and stories, getting the word out is in itself a beginning.

PERSEVERANCE. *Wowacintanka.* To persist, to strive in spite of difficulties.

Native Americans have certainly persevered, but yet they remain the underdogs due to many circumstances, as described by Leonard Crow Dog in 1995: "There are 30 million Blacks and fewer than two million of us. African-Americans live in big cities and have a lot of voting power, forming one big voting bloc. We are divided into some three hundred tribes scattered all over the continent. If we want to talk to one another we have to do it in English. We live far from the centers of power where decisions are made. So, we cannot make our influence felt."

"Whites say not to blame them, they aren't involved. It's their ancestors who did wrong. But they should be involved. They are living on our land. We are still third-class citizens. We are still invisible. Indians are in jail. Indians are starving. You should take some responsibility, not for what was, but for what is. We can't put all of you back on the Mayflower. So, we've got to live with one another as best we can… There are many good and understanding people. The only trouble is, there's not enough of them."

In *Hope in the Dark,* Solnit reminds us that the Indian wars are not over. "In recent years they have begun to win some things, some of the time, and now wars are mostly in the courts, in Congress, over textbooks, novels, museums, movies, mascots, as well as on and over the land." From being a dying race, these people are now the fastest growing segment of the population, according to the 2010 U.S. census. Native people are a growing force. We can support these ongoing struggles by contributing to organizations that work with them, such as Earth Justice, American Civil Liberties Union, and others (see chapter on Useful Organizations). We can contact our legislators to make our voices heard about specific issues such as funding for the Indian Health Service.

COMPASSION. *Waunsilapi.* To care, to sympathize.

We humans crave meaning and purpose in life. One way to find it is to connect to a cause larger than ourselves. Sometimes it's hard to know how best to make a difference, to spread opportunity around so folks can live up to their potential, flourish, grow, and make their contributions to the world.

Studies have shown that helping others improves our own mental and physical health and extends our life expectancy. Giving makes you feel better; it changes your brain chemistry, like social glue. It's important for those in need also to be empowered, to have a chance to pay forward and to give back. With this in mind, many of the ideas below are for readers both within and outside the Rosebud community.

FORTITUDE. *Cantewasake.* Strength of heart and mind.

Where we grow up, our lifestyle, and the opportunities we are given are influenced not only by ambition. Other factors include luck, health, parenting, genetics, and outside support. Help in various forms can make a huge difference, even when circumstances seem grim.

"Millions of people are trapped in the prison of poverty. It is time to set them free. Sometimes it falls upon a generation to be great. You can be that great generation."—Nelson Mandela.

Studies show that education and reading can make the biggest difference in combatting poverty. Programs where various ages mingle and interact have strengthened many communities. Older children reading to younger ones, the young reading to the elders, and some communities even have kids reading to dogs who don't judge their performance.

* Donate books to:

Rosebud Sioux Tribe Head Start, 725 Hospital Rd. Rosebud, South Dakota, 57570, (605-747-2391).

Sapa Un Catholic Academy (grades K-7) Box 499, St Francis, South Dakota, 57572, (605-747-2361).

* Volunteers could contact large suburban libraries, First Book, or Reach Out and Read for book donations.

GENEROSITY. *Canteyuke.* To give, share, to have a heart.

There are ways to incorporate giving into your daily lives so they are not a sacrifice but an opportunity and a pleasure. Giving with friends is more fun than giving alone. The power of social networks can make giving in groups easy and rewarding, Readers can document everything with photos and videos and tie every gift to a particular project.

Some ideas:

* Pledge a birthday: friends donate to a charity or a cause in honor of the birthday person.

* Dining for a purpose—get friends together for a pot luck dinner and donate the money that would have been spent eating out; then maybe do it monthly. Or have guests bring food for a food pantry. You could name your group and post on social media to help others start their own groups.

* Global Grandmothers group decided that when they get a gift for their own grandchildren they also give to someone in need.

* A men's poker night could donate winnings.

* Book clubs could incorporate a giving dimension, either money or books. Maybe donate the books after reading them. Native stories are especially appreciated.

* Use the web and social media fundraising strategies.

RESPECT. *Wawoohola.* To be considerate, to hold in high esteem.

Finding social purpose can help one's own social adjustment, transition and recovery. The act of supporting others somehow seems to be a step toward overcoming one's own injuries, as shown in models such as Alcoholics Anonymous (AA).

* Donate AA books to Rosebud's AA and substance abuse groups:

* St. Francis Mission, PO Box 499, St Francis, South Dakota, 57572.

* Rosebud Alcohol Treatment Program, 719 W. BIA, Rosebud, South Dakota, 57570.

Leaders of change are not the wealthiest or best-connected, but the most persistent. Progress arrives in incremental improvements. Goals must be practical to get results. Organizers must understand "the lay of the land." Leaders and followers all need to keep chipping away at poverty and injustice. People can hook into larger existing proven groups and expand their efforts, rather than spending time and energy starting new projects.

* The Linus Project donates baby blankets to hospitals.

Talent is universal, but opportunity is not. "Focus not on where someone is from but where that person is willing to go and whether he's willing to work constructively … There is no one way of doing things. We need to have large toolboxes and to lend and borrow tools freely." William De Buys, in *Hope in the Dark*, p.88.

WISDOM. *Woksape.* To understand what is right and true, to use knowledge well.

HONOR. *Wayuonihan.* To have integrity, an honest and upright character.

This book lists some useful organizations as a starting point. But if you find a nonprofit that appeals to you check it out on Charity Navigator, Charity Watch, or Guide Star, Better Business Bureau, or Wise Giving Alliance to make sure it's not a scam. Check the FTC website: ftc.gov/charityfraud. Be wary of charities and organizations—research them as you would in making a large purchase. Of all the money donated in America, only about one third goes to the needy. Some goes to the underfunded arts and universities, plus overhead: administration, computers, training, and marketing. Some overhead is necessary to use the money efficiently. Go where your heart directs you but don't forget your brain. There is good evidence about what does work and make a difference.

SACRIFICE. *Icicupi.* To give of oneself, an offering.

*Donate: Give money, materials, time, blood. Become an organ donor.

*Volunteer: Get involved with your time and skills. Make it a social event and volunteer with friends. One time, or on a regular basis. Check out resources such as RSVP.org, idealist.org, mentor.org for ideas.

*Advocate: Speaking up for the voiceless can be just as lifesaving as medicine. Spread the word to hold the government and its elected officials accountable. The Washington *Post* declared on 1/9/17 that

"1960s-style protest is back," Use both politics as well as outside advocacy and organizing groups. Write and call your members of Congress, write letters to the editor.

* Results.org is a platform for advocacy you can tap into – you don't have to start from scratch. Many advocacy groups have a social media presence these days, with pleas for action, formatted letters, petitions and speaking points.

BRAVERY. *Woohitike.* A meaningful life isn't a destination but a journey.

"If you don't like the news… go out and make some of your own" newsman Wes Nisker proclaimed in the 1970s. Marchers and protesters have been rallying around the world to support various causes. In the fall of 2016 the water protectors at the Dakota Pipeline attracted worldwide attention and support, with thousands of people at their camp in North Dakota.

"First, they ignore you, then laugh at you, then fight you. Then you win." said Gandhi, regarding change. But these stages unfold slowly. There is no single answer or path, but many ways to help, depending on your interests and background. There is a need not just for technical answers but for greater empathy and support. People also need the power of opportunity, and of perseverance and patience.

HUMILITY. *Unsiiciyapi.* To be humble, modest, unpretentious.

Every act is an act of faith, because you don't know what will happen. You just hope and use whatever wisdom and experience seems most likely to get you to your goal, according to Solnit. There is good reason to have hope. Our acts count. We are making history all the time. Innovations often begin with simple changes. We must look back to get a perspective to see and measure progress, or sometimes to see that we have at least kept something from getting worse. "We are all activists in some way or another, because both our actions and inactions have impact." —Rebecca Solnit.

LOVE. *Cantognake.* To place and hold in one's heart.

"If you do good you feel good…Participating in a cause larger than yourself builds up our social networks, creates a sense of fulfillment, gets us out of bed, and helps make a difference in the lives of others—

even as it affirms a purpose for our own lives on earth." Kristoff and WuDunn from *A Path Appears*, p 315.

A wise Lakota man once said, "A single bee is ignored. But when millions come together even the bravest run in fear."

4 things you can do in the next 5 minutes:

1.   Email friends to invite them to a monthly giving circle, to explore powerful ways to make a difference. Keep it fun by including refreshments.

2.   Consider supporting an early childhood program, such as collecting books or sponsoring a child through a program such as Save the Children.

3.   Become an advocate. On *www.results.org* you can sign up to join lobbying efforts to get Congress to pay more attention to poverty at home and abroad.

4.   Register to donate your organs upon your death, saving the lives of up to eight other people. You can register when you renew your driver's license or at *www.organdonor.gov*.

Consider this an invitation, as a gateway to open a path to a better life, for yourself and for others. We can work together to make Rosebud and other communities less tragic and more magic.

17. Useful organizations and support

his book lists some useful organizations as a starting point, but if you find a nonprofit that appeals to you check it out on Charity Navigator, Charity Watch, or Guide Star, Better Business Bureau, Wise Giving Alliance to make sure it's not a scam.

Government:

Members of the United States Congress—GovTrack.us

https://www.govtrack.us/congress/members

Use GovTrack to find out who represents you in Congress and what bills they're working on, or select a state to list all *senators and representatives* from that state.

Local resources:

Rosebud Hospital—Baby hats, shirts, onesies, and blankets are always welcome—400 Soldier Creek Rd., Rosebud, South Dakota, 57570, (605)-747-2231.

Soldier Woman Art & Gift Gallery: *www.soldierwomangallery.com*
Hwy 83 S Mission, SD 57555, (605) 856-4774.

Shop online and in the store—local artisans fine Lakota crafts and art. We feature jewelry created by owner Linda Szabo and husband Paul Szabo, star quilts, wall hangings, home décor beadwork, quillwork, shawls, pottery, prints, cards, music, T-shirts, dream catchers, moccasins, supplies and much more.

Sinte Gleska University: *www.sintegleska.edu*, (605) 856-8100; Mail: P.O. Box 105, Mission, South Dakota, 57555; Shipping: 101 Antelope Lake Circle, Mission, South Dakota, 57555.

Rosebud Sioux Tribe
RST Head Start—accepts books, toys. 725 Hospital Rd., Rosebud, South Dakota, 57570, (605) 747-2391.

Rosebud Alcohol Treatment Program—accepts AA books.
7 Hospital Lane, Rosebud, South Dakota, 57570 (605) 747-2342.

Saint Francis Mission—accepts AA books, schoolbooks K-7.
www.sfmission.org; P.O. Box 499, 350 Oak St. St. Francis, South Dakota, 57572; Phone: (605) 747-236.

Programs: Religious Education, *Sapa Un* Academy, Lakota Studies, Alcohol and Drug Recovery, Suicide Prevention, KINI Radio, Dental Clinic, Museum, Inculturation Project

St. Francis Mission prides itself on programs that promote a healthy Catholic church and address the difficult issues the Lakota people face. Every program started at the Mission in the last eight years is directed by a Lakota person. Each and every program is designed to further Lakota leadership and champion Lakota and Catholic values.

St. Francis Indian School *sfisk12.org*; 502 East Warrior Dr., P.O. Box 379, St Francis, South Dakota, 57572 (605) 747-2299.

Private non-sectarian school serving grades PK-12.

Environment:

Earth Justice: *earthjustice.org*.

Earthjustice has been the legal backbone for thousands of organizations, large and small. As the nation's original and largest nonprofit environmental law organization, we leverage our expertise and commitment to fight for justice and advance the promise of a healthy world for all. We represent every one of our clients free of charge.

Friends of the Earth: *foe.org*.

Friends of the Earth strives for a healthier and more just world. We understand that the challenges facing our planet call for more than half measures, so we push for the reforms that are needed, not merely the ones that are politically easy. We are one of a global network representing more than two million activists in 75 different countries. In the United States, we advocate in the halls of Congress, in state capitals, and with community groups around the country. We urge policymakers to defend the environment and work towards a healthy environment for all people.

Friends of the Earth seeks to change the perception of the public, media and policy makers—and effect policy change—with hard-hitting, well-reasoned policy analysis and advocacy campaigns that describe what needs to be done, rather than what is seen as politically feasible or politically correct. This hard-hitting advocacy has been the key to our successful campaigns over our 47-year history.

One way that Friends of the Earth works to achieve a just and healthy world, is by focusing on the economic drivers that are encouraging environmental degradation. Depending on the issue, these drivers may include public investment, granting corporations the right to pollute, or other factors. With key policy expertise at the federal and state levels, Friends of the Earth works to eliminate these drivers and thus bring environmental degradation to a halt.

Next Gen Climate Action: *Nextgenclimate.org*.
We fight to protect our earth, our civil rights, and our future.

NRDC Action Fund: *Nrdcactionfund.org*.
The NRDC Action Fund's mission is to build political support in the United States for protecting the planet and its people. We mobilize influential constituencies, experts, community leaders and others to directly advocate for clean air and water, public health, biodiversity, and a stable climate. We support candidates who stand up for environmental protection, and we expose those who side with polluters rather than the public good. We encourage people from across the country to join us in our efforts.

Public Health and Social Organizations:

Habitat for Humanity: *Habitat.org*.
Habitat for Humanity is a nonprofit housing organization working locally and in nearly 1,400 communities across the United States and in approximately 70 countries around the world. Habitat's vision is of a world where everyone has a decent place to live. Habitat works toward this vision by building and improving homes in partnership with individuals and families in need of a decent and affordable place to live.

Local contact is Sicangu Tikaga Okiciyapi HFH, P.O. Box 327, Mission, South Dakota, 57555; (605) 856-2665.

Job Corps: *jobcorps.gov*; (800) 733-5627.

Job Corps is a free education and training program that helps young people learn a career, earn a high school diploma or GED, and find and keep a good job. For eligible young people at least 16 years of age that qualify as low income, Job Corps provides the all-around skills needed to succeed in a career and in life.

Americorps: *Nationalservice.gov.*

AmeriCorps programs do more than move communities forward; they serve their members by creating jobs and providing pathways to opportunity for young people entering the workforce. AmeriCorps places thousands of young adults into intensive service positions where they learn valuable work skills, earn money for education, and develop an appreciation for citizenship.

Alcoholics Anonymous, Alanon, Alateen: *aa.org.*

Alcoholics Anonymous is an international fellowship of men and women who have had a drinking problem. It is nonprofessional, self-supporting, multiracial, apolitical, and available almost everywhere. There are no age or education requirements. Membership is open to anyone who wants to do something about his or her drinking problem.

ACLU: *ACLU.org.*

For nearly 100 years, the ACLU has been our nation's guardian of liberty, working in courts, legislatures, and communities to defend and preserve the individual rights and liberties that the Constitution and the laws of the United States guarantee everyone in this country.

Amnesty International: *Amnestyusa.org.*

Amnesty International is a global movement of millions of people demanding human rights for all people—no matter who they are or where they are. We are the world's largest grassroots human rights organization. We work to protect people wherever justice, freedom, truth, and dignity are denied.

Children's Defense Fund: *www.childrensdefense.org.*

The Children's Defense Fund (CDF) is a 501(c)(3) non-profit child advocacy organization that has worked relentlessly for more than 40 years to ensure a level playing field for all children. We champion policies and programs that lift children out of poverty; protect them from abuse and neglect; and ensure their access to health care, quality education and a moral and spiritual foundation. Supported by foundation and corporate grants and individual donations, CDF advocates nationwide on behalf of children to ensure children are always a priority.

We are a national organization with the capacity to work for children at federal, state and community levels across the country. We have our headquarters in Washington, D.C., and offices in California, Minnesota, Mississippi, New York, Ohio, South Carolina and Texas. Through these offices, we expand our work into North Dakota, South Dakota, Iowa, Alabama, Georgia, Arkansas, Louisiana and New Jersey. CDF Haley Farm in Clinton, Tenn., is our home for spiritual renewal, character and leadership development, intergenerational mentoring, and interracial and interfaith dialog about children's issues.

RAINN – Rape, Abuse, Incest National Network. *www.rainn.org.*

RAINN (Rape, Abuse & Incest National Network) is the nation's largest anti-sexual violence organization. RAINN created and operates the National Sexual Assault Hotline, (800) 656-HOPE, in partnership with more than 1,000 local sexual assault service providers across the country and operates the DoD Safe Helpline for the Department of Defense. RAINN also carries out programs to prevent sexual violence, help victims, and ensure that perpetrators are brought to justice.

National Indian Health Board: *www.nihb.org.*

910 Pennsylvania Avenue SE, Washington, D.C., 20003; (202) 507-4070.

Founded in 1972, NIHB is a 501(c) 3 not for profit, charitable organization providing health care advocacy services, facilitating Tribal budget consultation and providing timely information, and other services to all Tribal governments. NIHB also conducts research, provides policy analysis, program assessment and development, national and regional meeting planning, training, technical assistance, program and project management. NIHB presents the Tribal perspective while monitoring, reporting on and responding to federal legislation and regulations. It also serves as conduit to open opportunities for the advancement of American Indian and Alaska Native health care with other national and international organizations, foundations corporations and others in its quest to build support for, and advance, Indian health care issues.

National Suicide Prevention Lifeline

We can all help prevent suicide. The Lifeline provides 24/7, free and confidential support for people in distress, prevention and crisis resources for you or your loved ones, and best practices for professionals. (800) 273-8255.

Education:

American Indian College Fund: *collegefund.org.*

Founded in 1989, supports Native student access to higher education through scholarship programs. Mission is to transform lives and communities.

Reach out and read.org

Incorporates books into pediatric care and encourages families to read aloud together

Epilogue

19 70s Rosebud set the stage for several of us who met there to fully embrace life elsewhere. Judy did move to the Kelly dairy farm in tiny Fultonville, New York, with Russell, and they have expanded it to be one of the largest in the area. They have both been innovative leaders in the community, to the extent that Hillary Clinton visited to interview them about farming issues when she was running for the New York senate. They took their three teenaged sons with their church youth group back to Rosebud for a week of community service in 1998. Judy became a family nurse practitioner, running her own rural clinic for many years. She retired in 2017 to travel, write her own stories and play with her growing brood of grandchildren on the farm.

Stephanie served in the Peace Corps in Honduras before becoming a nurse midwife and recently retired from working in West Virginia. Our little squash garden in Rosebud was only the beginning, as she is now a master gardener. She visits her daughter and granddaughter in Florida as often as possible.

Rose left Rosebud to be the only medical person on an ice floe in the arctic, the first free-world winter expedition charting currents in the Beaufort Sea. While she was there, the ice floe broke down the middle of the mess tent, splitting their camp – twice! She married one of the ice scientists, Norm Braz. They have three grown children, and they're living happily in Wyoming. Rose also earned her Masters' degree in nursing, spending several years as a Quality Assurance analyst.

Dr. Steve Tosi is the head of the urology department at the UMASS Medical School. His first wife, Terry died of cancer. He has two grown children, and travels with his wife of thirty years, Lindsey, when they are not home enjoying their small farm with six cows, several goats and chickens. He started writing his own book about Rosebud entitled "Federal Health Care, With Reservations." He says that "Rosebud was a phenomenal experience. We probably feel that way because we survived."

Charlie White and George Whirlwind Soldier, the Physicians Assistants whom Dr. Tosi trained, sadly have both now passed away. At George's recent memorial he was remembered as a caring man and a role model for many in the community.

Lorna Her Many Horses still lives in Rosebud near many of her children and enjoys keeping everyone in line whenever possible.

Susan Beeson is retired and enjoying gardening, travel, and outdoor activities with her husband outside Chicago.

Wanda Big Crow passed away in 2011.

I became a nurse practitioner in gerontology, publishing research articles on advance directives and on memory issues. I worked to help change legislation for nurse practitioners when I lived in North Carolina, and again when we moved to Pennsylvania, helping to form a Nurse Practitioner group which has now grown to several hundred members. I retired in Maryland in 2014, with our two children and their growing families nearby. I sometimes share these stories and other memoirs when my family gathers for Sunday dinner. Our friend Pam who visited me twice in Rosebud now lives down the street from us and still has big Italian parties. My husband Tom and I play tennis, some music, and enjoy travelling to collect more stories to tell.

Many of our friendships have endured, especially between Judy, Stephanie, and myself, as we have gathered many times over the years to laugh, reminisce, and to make new memories. In March of 2015 we reconnected and met with Steve Tosi to swap stories and to share more memories and laughs. In April 2016, Rose joined Judy and Steph at my house to rekindle our connections too. The brief Rosebuddy reunion proved to be a remarkable event in itself after more than forty years. Judy and Rose had not met since their brief overlap in 1974, but we all embraced and mingled seamlessly. We compared our versions of the old stories in this book, laughing and reflecting. Some of the intervening years were filled in, and a few new memories were created to cherish. We had an art night, painting rosebuds with local friends eager to meet the infamous Rosebuddies. We each started knitting various prayer shawls to donate to Rosebud Hospital patients, or staff, as Native flute music softly set the mood. We cherish not only the friendships, but also the strength and confidence that Rosebud ultimately gave us all, to pursue advanced nursing degrees, to mentor new nurses and to pay it forward. We veterans of Rosebud look back on our remarkable careers and have been blessed with extraordinary lives.

33. R: Nancy, Lorna Her Many Horses, and Steph at the Turtle Creek Café.
S: Rosebuddies reunion 2016: Steph, Judi, Nancy and Rose.

34. Rosebuddies Stephanie, Nancy and Judy, with 3 buds on a rosebush.

Further information:

Books:

Bury My Heart at Wounded Knee by Dee Brown, Bantam Book, NY, NY, 1972.

Lame Deer, Seeker of Visions by John (Fire) Lame Deer and Richard Erodes, Simon and Schuster, NY, NY 1972.

Lakota Woman by Mary Crow Dog and Richard Erodes, Harper and Collins, NY, NY, 1990.

Black Elk Speaks as told through John Niehardt (Flaming Rainbow), University of Nebraska Press, Lincoln, NE, 1961.

Spotted Tail's Folk by George Hyde, University of Oklahoma Press, Norman, OK, 1961.

Custer Died for Your Sins: An Indian Manifesto by V. Deloria, Jr., Macmillan, NY, NY, 1969.

Neither Wolf nor Dog by Kent Norburn, New World Library, Noveto, CA, 2009

The Heart of Everything That Is: The Untold Story of Red Cloud, An American Legend by B. Drury and T. Clavin, Simon and Schuster, NY, NY, 2014.

In the Spirit of Crazy Horse by Peter Matthiesssen, Viking Press, NY, NY, 1983.

The Broken Cord by Michael Dorris, Harper and Row, NY, NY, 1989.

Where White Men Fear to Tread: The Autobiography of Russell Means by Russell Means with Marvin J. Wolf, St. Martin's Griffin, New York, 1995.

Rosebud Sioux Images of America by D. Sprague, Arcadia Publishing, Charleston, SC, 2005

Crow Dog: Four Generations of Sioux Medicine Men by Leonard Crow Dog and Richard Erodes, Harper Perennial, NY, 1995.

The Lakota Way: Stories and Lessons for Living by Joseph Marshall III, Penguin Compass, NY, NY, 2001.

Wounded Knee 1973: Still Bleeding by Stew Magnuson, Court Bridge Publishing, Arlington, VA, 2013.

A Path Appears by N. D. Kristoff and S. WuDunn, Vintage Books, New York, 2014.

Hope in the Dark by Rebecca Solnitt, Haymarket Books, Chicago, IL, 2016.

So Rich So Poor by P. Edelman, New York Press, New York, NY, 2012.

The Price of a Gift: A Lakota Healer's Story by G. Mohatt and J. Eagle Elk, University of Nebraska Press, Lincoln, NE, 2000.

Life's Journey – Zuya: Oral Teachings from Rosebud by Albert White Hat, Sr., University of Utah Press, 2012.

Plagues, Politics, and Policy: A Chronicle of the Indian Health Service ...

https://www.amazon.com/Plagues-Politics-Policy-Chronicle-1955.../0739146033

Plagues, Politics, and Policy: A Chronicle of the *Indian Health Service*, 1955-2008: 9780739146033: Medicine & Health Science *Books* @ Amazon.com.

Films:

Thunderheart

Dances with Wolves

Smoke Signals

Avatar

The Revenant

Awake, A Dream from Standing Rock

Wind River

Government Publications:

Information on Rosebud Service Unit by HEW / PHS/ Indian Health Service, Aberdeen Area, 1972

Health Care Crisis at Rosebud, American Indian Research Project by Allen and Allen, 1973

Photo Index

Acknowledgements

S o many people contributed to the completion of this book. First, the Lakota People of Rosebud who touched my life, and some of whose tales I tell. Next, I must thank Judy Niederwerfer Kelly, my original Rosebuddy. Stephanie (last name withheld on request) also has laughed and reminisced with us over the years, rehearsing the stories into our memory banks. I couldn't have made the return trip without her. Steve Tosi, with whom we reconnected after forty-plus years has shared our enthusiasm and contributed some of his own remarkable stories. Rose Rouch Braz has shared some humdinger stories too.

My new Rosebud Team—was so welcoming and helpful: Denise One Star, Maxine Bordeaux, Gina One Star, Cynthia Crow Eagle. Sandra Black Bear, Lorna and Kathi Her Many Horses, and Jody Waln. Maxine Bordeaux has been especially helpful as my cultural consultant and local contact in Rosebud, with crucial information and feedback.

Connie Wones is the memoir writing teacher who helped me begin this book and has been very generous with editorial advice. Our writing group, which continued when the memoir class ended, has listened to all the unpolished stories as they came off the press, and offered feedback and support to carry on. Julie Castillo, another writing teacher who coached me to begin the publication process. My friends and family who were privy to early drafts and were interested enough to ask questions, helped me greatly to know where to clarify, add details and cheer me on.

And of course, Tom, my wonderful patient husband and tech support, who has heard the tales many times over the years, but his encouragement and support never waver.

About the author

Nancy Palker has retired from nursing and lives in Maryland with her husband and nearby family. Her career spanned more than forty-five years in health care as an aide, registered nurse and nurse practitioner in gerontology, working with several ethnic groups. She organized nursing groups and successfully worked for changes in health care legislation and regulation in several states. She has presented her research at national and local events, has taught health topics to professional and senior groups, and has accompanied a musical group of 200 teenagers through Europe as their nurse. She continues to advocate for improvements in Rosebud's health care system.

Made in the USA
Middletown, DE
19 March 2019